GET OFF
THE DIME

GET OFF THE DIME

The Secret of Changing Who Pays for Your Health Care

SREEDHAR POTARAZU M.D., M.B.A.

TRINITY PRESS

South New York, NY

Published by
Trinity Press
South New York, NY

Publisher's Cataloging-in-Publication Data
Potarazu, Sreedhar.

Get off the dime : the secret of changing who pays for your health care / by Sreedhar Potarazu. – South New York, NY : Trinity Press, 2009.

  p. ; cm.

  ISBN: 978-0-9822113-0-4

  1. Medical care—United States. 2. Public health—United States. I. Title.

  RA395.A3 P67 2009
  362.1–dc22   2008940249

Project coordination by Jenkins Group, Inc.
Interior design by Brooke Camfield
www.BookPublishing.com

Printed in the United States of America
13 12 11 10 09 • 5 4 3 2 1

Sandeep . . .The eternal light within all of us.

Contents

LIST OF GRAPHICS

PREFACE

This book is a call to action for anyone in this country who pays for health care using the current health-care-purchasing system. Employers and employees have been at a disadvantage for far too long when it comes to understanding how they can use technology to improve the cost and quality of their health care. There simply isn't enough transparency in the system to help health-care consumers make informed decisions.

This became apparent to me when I was studying for my MBA in the late 1990s. I was practicing medicine as an ophthalmologist with a focus on diseases that affect the optic nerve, specifically neuro-ophthalmology and glaucoma. During medical school and my residency, I'd been interested in the business aspects of medicine. But even as a fellow at the Bascom Palmer Eye Institute at the University of Miami and later as a faculty member at Johns Hopkins University, I thought I could do more to improve the business of medicine.

During my MBA course work, I started to dig deeper into understanding basic business principles, and I became intrigued with the idea of consumerism and how sophisticated we've become in our purchasing habits. Whether cars, computers, clothes, or books, we're able to use technology to become more empowered consumers. But why hasn't this same approach worked for health care? Why haven't we been able to realize the same improvements in the cost and quality of health care that we have in every other segment of the economy?

Then, one day, it dawned on me that in health care, the purchaser of services hadn't been empowered. Instead of starting at the top of the health-care supply chain, the primary focus for health-care reform had been with health-care providers—but change needs to start at the top and with those who pay for health-care services. It also became apparent that technology could be the catalyst for providing the transparency employers and employees needed in order to become more sophisticated health-care purchasers.

That idea was a springboard to launching a software company based on leveraging the power of the Internet to drive information. As the business grew, I had many opportunities to interact with business leaders from across the country, and I gained a unique health-care perspective. As an ophthalmologist, I spent seven years delivering care to my patients, and I spent an equal number of years understanding how companies make decisions about the health benefits they provide for their employees. This gave me a 180-degree perspective of how dollars flow through the health-care system, from the entity subsidizing it to the entity providing the care.

My impetus for writing this book is to help health-care purchasers understand the economics of how health care is purchased, especially in the current economic environment. I believe that the paradigm will begin to change once purchasers understand how the system really works and once they gain greater transparency into the services they are purchasing. This approach mirrors the visibility consumers have in other sectors of the economy by leveraging technology to help drive improvements in the cost and quality of goods and services.

There are four important messages in this book.

First, cost and quality can improve if employers and employees have access to the right technology and the proper metrics that will provide transparency into health-care costs and quality.

Second, because technology is the best method for delivering insight into the metrics, its adoption needs to be pervasive throughout the health-care supply chain. Incentives are needed to speed the use of technology for this purpose.

Third, we need to help disintermediate the inefficiencies that have existed in the health-care system as a result of a lack of transparency between those who are paying for health care and those who are delivering the care. Physicians will also benefit from better transparency into cost and quality if purchasers can deal directly with them.

Fourth, it's important to recognize that health is measured not by the cost of illness but by the cost of *people with illness* because this is what drives the impact of health care on society. The goal should be to ensure that the American workforce is not only healthy but also healthy and productive because that productivity is what will lead to better economic performance for each company—and the entire country.

The title of this book, *Get off the Dime*, was chosen as a call to action because the time has come for employers and employees to take control of their health care to drive change throughout the health-care system. Visibility into the right metrics will enable this change.

It's interesting to note that one of the first times "get off the dime" appeared in *The New York Times* was in 1943, as a quote from a labor leader about the complacency of the War Labor Board prior to a worker strike. As you'll soon learn, labor unions played a pivotal role in strengthening the concept of employer-sponsored health care by including benefits as an accepted part of union collective bargaining.

Get off the Dime is now a call to corporate America and its workforce to recognize their dual roles in changing the current approach to employer-sponsored health care. Employers and their employees working together can be a significant catalyst for improving the cost and quality of health care because that is from where the dollars begin to flow and for whom there is the most to gain.

The financial meltdown of the fall of 2008 has created an even greater sense of urgency to fix health care. The single most common cause for personal bankruptcy is an individual who cannot pay for health care. In an environment where governments across the world have stepped in to provide stability to weakening banking systems, the resources and financing available to transform health care are shrinking.

New leadership in the White House will be significantly challenged to take on the financial responsibility of effectively transforming the health-care system. In many ways, the debacle of the banking system, with the lack of oversight in derivatives and credit swaps, superimposed on the mortgage meltdown, mirrors the impending collapse of the U.S. health-care system, in terms of the lack of transparency that exists as to how dollars flow in the system. It is time for the market to awaken before the next crisis hits. At that point, there will be little recourse or time for purchasers of health care to "Get off the Dime."

Sreedhar Potarazu, M.D., M.B.A.
McLean, Virginia

ACKNOWLEDGMENTS

My gratitude to my family for their ever-constant love and support.
My humble respects to all of the many mentors for their guidance.
My appreciation to friends and colleagues for their loyalty and faith.
My reverence to all the Great Souls that have paved the way for the world to understand and accept a new generation of leaders like President Barack Obama.

May the blessings of the Lord flow through us to the world around us.

CHAPTER 1

A Brief History of Employer-Sponsored Health Insurance

"Give me health and a day, and I will make the pomp of emperors ridiculous."

—Ralph Waldo Emerson

I f you've dealt with any aspect of health-care costs during the past several years, you don't need an ophthalmologist to help you see that this country's approach to delivering health care is out of focus. Much research has been conducted and mountains of data have been compiled to reinforce what we already know. The United States spends more on health per capita than any other country.[1] In 2007, health-care spending represented 16 percent of the U.S. gross domestic product (GDP); this is expected to reach almost 20 percent of the GDP by 2016.[2] Continuing at its current rate, national health spending is anticipated to reach $4.2 trillion at that time.

One would expect, for such a significant investment, that every man, woman, and child in the country would be able to receive the health-care services that he or she needs. Some calculate that if the money were pooled, we could afford to hire a physician for every seven families.[3] Unfortunately, our national health-care bill doesn't necessarily translate into higher-quality health care or even higher access to health care. Despite a health spending price tag in the trillions, the percentage of the population under 65 without any health insurance coverage is about 17 percent.[4] These 40 million Americans do not receive needed services because they can't afford them.[5]

The majority of those who are fortunate to have health insurance— about 158 million nonelderly Americans—receive coverage through their place of employment.[6] The Kaiser Family Foundation and Health Research and Educational Trust reports that 60 percent of employers offered health insurance coverage in 2007; however, as impressive as this figure may first appear, the number of employers offering coverage has decreased from 69 percent in 2000.[7]

Because small businesses couldn't sustain double-digit premium increases, business owners had to make the decision to either drop health insurance coverage or drop out of business. Rising premium

3

rates are tied to an increase in health-care spending that includes rising provider fees, inpatient and outpatient hospital services, technological advances, pharmaceutical breakthroughs, taxes, inflation, and the accompanying inefficiencies that are a natural by-product of the current cumbersome system of providing health care.

Employers' contributions to their employees' health-care coverage amounts to about 25 percent of total spending, which is more than $440 billion.[8] With this in mind, there's no doubt that many of the country's employers would prefer not to be the benefactors of health benefits to their workers.

In fact, many business leaders believe that health-care costs threaten our country's ability to be competitive in the global economy.[9] Employers in the United States have seen a steep increase in the percentage of payroll for health benefits in the past 40 years, from 1.2 percent of payroll to almost 10 percent.[10] When compared with those in other countries, American employers contribute more to health benefits than many of our top trading partners, putting the country at a disadvantage in a decidedly competitive global market.

How did American employers get saddled with the burden of providing health insurance benefits to millions? That question has no easy answer because the roots of employer-sponsored health-care plans are connected to the federal government, unions, and the IRS.

Employer-Sponsored Health Benefits: The First 100 Years

Winston Churchill has often been quoted as saying, "The further backwards you look, the further forward you can see."[11] His statement is especially relevant for examining the milestones in the evolution of

4

employer-sponsored health insurance in the United States. Before we can evaluate methods for helping employers better manage their health-care costs in the future, we need to gain an understanding of how health benefits became tied to one's employment in the first place.

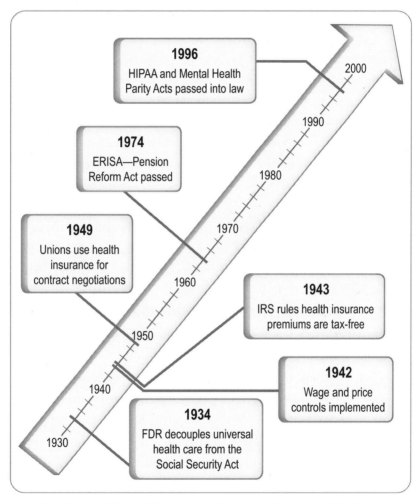

1.1 Timeline of Major Milestones in Employer-Sponsored Health-Care

As early as 1916, legislation for compulsory insurance was presented by a number of states, and other states appointed commissions to study the problem. In an article published in *The New York Times*, the author berated the country for its lack of an insurance system for the sick. "In this matter America has the dubious distinction of standing alone. Every other important industrial nation has in force some form of health insurance subsidized by the Government."[12]

It seemed inevitable that some day employers would accept the responsibility for providing health-care benefits for their employees. With the goal to create laws to protect workers' on-the-job health and safety, the American Association for Labor Legislation submitted proposals for compulsory health insurance. Those proposals didn't gain traction at the time because of opposition from sectors that could have embraced it: physicians, pharmacists, and commercial insurance companies.[13]

Instead, the evolution of employer-sponsored health benefits in the United States was driven by the premise of enabling companies to gain a competitive advantage for recruiting and retaining employees. When health care was added as an employee benefit in the 1940s, it was considered a creative approach for optimizing productivity and enhancing global competitive advantage. However, few at the time could foresee the repercussions it would have for employers in the future.

When President Franklin D. Roosevelt decided against including universal health care as part of his New Deal, he unknowingly put the country's employers on the path to providing health benefits to their employees and retirees and their dependents. In 1934, he bowed to pressure from several influential physicians and the then-powerful American Medical Association (AMA) when he decoupled universal health care from the Social Security Act in order to assure its passage.[14]

The Social Security Act was signed into law on August 14, 1935. Without a national health-care plan in place, private insurers such as Blue Cross and Blue Shield adopted a model for providing hospital coverage to individuals. Commercial insurance followed soon after.

Employer-sponsored insurance would take on an increasingly important role during World War II, when demand for a limited pool of workers was high. On April 27, 1942, President Roosevelt implemented wage and price controls to restrict companies from using pay as an unfair advantage to attract employees. Wages may have been frozen, but employers were allowed to add to their worker benefits. Health insurance attracted workers, and employer-sponsored health care was born.

In 1943, the Internal Revenue Service issued a ruling that helped advance the popularity of employer-sponsored health insurance. The IRS ruling gave employers permission to continue paying health insurance premiums in pretax dollars and made benefits tax free for employees. The IRS helped drive demand for health insurance again in 1954 when it ruled that employer contributions to employee health plans shouldn't be part of an employee's taxable income.

Labor unions also played a part in strengthening the concept of employer-sponsored health care by including benefits as an accepted part of union collective bargaining. One ruling by the War Labor Board in 1945 restricted employers from making changes to insurance plans before a labor contract period expired. Another ruling in 1949 added pension and insurance benefits to the definition of employee wages, thus allowing unions to use health insurance as part of their contract negotiations.

Between 1940 and 1960, the number of people enrolled in health insurance plans surged from 12.3 to 122.5 million Americans.[15] "Government policies that promoted a link between health insurance and employment lowered the real price of health insurance and further stimulated demand in the 1940s and 1950s."[16]

7

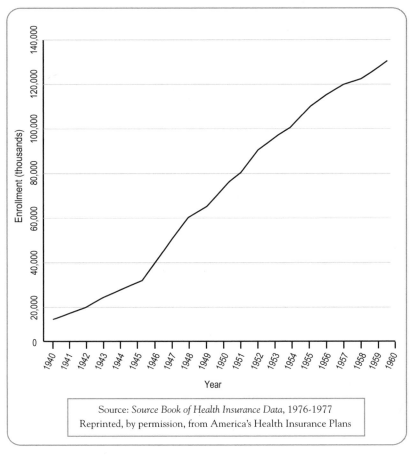

Source: *Source Book of Health Insurance Data*, 1976-1977
Reprinted, by permission, from America's Health Insurance Plans

1.2   Number of People Enrolled in Health Insurance Plans, 1940-1960

When Harry S. Truman was elected president in 1945, he spent part of his first term in office resurrecting the idea of a national health insurance plan, but he faced strong resistance to what was referred to as "socialized medicine" by his opponents. In addition, company-sponsored health insurance was so well entrenched in the country that it made the struggle for government-sponsored health insurance all the more difficult.

Twenty years later, on July 30, 1965, President Lyndon B. Johnson signed the Social Security Amendments into law, creating Medicare and Medicaid. Medicare (the program providing health insurance coverage for individuals 65 and over) and Medicaid (the program for insuring the economically disadvantaged) became the government's primary entrance into health-care finance. It was fitting for former President Truman to attend the signing and receive the first Medicare card.[17]

Outside Influences Affect Health Insurance

Medicare and Medicaid were the primary, but by no means the only, ways in which the federal government became involved in the field of health-care finance.

The Employee Retirement Income Security Act of 1974 (ERISA), also called the Pension Reform Act, was another milestone in employer-sponsored health care, although it wasn't intended as such. The purpose of the federal law was to set standards for pension and health plans to protect employees enrolled in the plans. In essence, it gave self-insured employers an exemption from state mandates, allowing them more flexibility in designing the health insurance plans for their employees.

ERISA had several unintended effects: (1) it created a challenge for states wanting to implement a universal health-care model because ERISA overrode states' rights and (2) it undermined the insurance system because employers with a large number of employees were able to remove healthy employees from risk pools, essentially making insurance coverage more difficult for smaller employers.

The tax code for ERISA continues to favor employees, giving them a tax break for health-care costs that are paid by their employers. Employers also receive a tax break in the form of not having to pay payroll taxes on the provided health-care benefits.

Companies were also affected by the Statement of Financial Accounting Standards 106, released by the Financial Accounting Standards Board (FASB) in 1990. This change in accounting rules required companies to stop measuring the cost of providing health-care benefits to retirees on a cash basis and switch to recording their future obligation. This modification had a significant impact on companies' financial statements and caused many to retool their retiree plans while others simply eliminated them.

The Shift from Fee-for-Service to Managed Care

The model for pre-1980s health benefits was based on fee-for-service (FFS) plans that allowed employees and their covered dependents to seek care from the providers of their choice without preadmission certification. With FFS plans, also known as indemnity plans, either patients were reimbursed for the cost of services or providers and facilities were paid directly. Between 1988 and 1989, health insurance premiums rose by an average of 18 percent,[18] and the economics of these conventional plans could not be sustained.

During this time of rising premiums, a major shift occurred in the approach to health benefits when employers began favoring managed-care plans over the conventional FFS plans. Managed-care plans, such as health maintenance organizations (HMOs) and preferred provider organizations (PPOs), were created to contain health-care costs by limiting health-care access to a network of contracted providers. Employees and their dependents had fewer provider and facility choices and were required to have approval for specialty care.

In 1993, President Bill Clinton made another attempt at passing universal health-care legislation; however, as with past presidential health-care-reform efforts, the plan was met with resistance from Congress. Some believed that the plan would be too expensive to implement, and others thought that it required too much government regulation. Even though compromises to the initial plan were made, they were also defeated.

Several positive efforts at smaller reforms were made. In 1996, Congress passed the Health Insurance Portability and Accountability Act (HIPAA) to help individuals retain their health insurance when moving between jobs and offered protection for those with preexisting conditions. That same year, Congress signed into law the Mental Health Parity Act, which required that mental health benefits be equal to the annual dollar amounts for medical and surgical benefits for those group health plans that offer such benefits.

Health-Care-Reform Redux

A comprehensive system for providing health care in this country has been part of the political debate since the early 1900s. In those days, many opposed compulsory health care, calling it "un-American." Others have referred to health insurance as "private social security."[19] It's safe to say that efforts at health-care reform will continue.

For almost 70 years, U.S. employers have understood the importance of providing health benefits to their employees in order to recruit and retain a world-class workforce. Employers in this country know that they can't compete in a global marketplace on the basis of compensation alone. If they want to survive—and thrive—in a global economy, they'll need to continue offering health benefits. In the twenty-first century, a strategic advantage for employers will be providing their employees with access to high-quality health care at a reasonable cost.

Simply put, employers will not be able to get out of the business of providing benefits if they want to remain in business. This was apparent even in 1916 when *The New York Times* rationalized to its readers that "the employer's contribution is justified broadly by the fact that it is profitable to him to maintain and improve the health of his employees."[20]

Chapter 1—Key Messages

- Prior to 1942, employees were on their own when it came time to take care of their health concerns. Once health-care benefits became tied to employment, employees became tied to their employers.

- Health-care costs represent a significant cost burden to companies wanting to remain competitive in a global economy.

- With the rising cost of health care and the impact on the workforce, the system of employer-sponsored health care is severely challenged.

- Companies that opt out of providing health insurance coverage risk losing skilled employees; those who continue to provide coverage risk declining profits.

- The inherent business of managing benefits requires an understanding of finance, health care, and technology to adequately determine the real effect.

- The ultimate outcome of how the system responds will depend on the empowering of two important constituents: employers and employees.

Chapter 1—Endnotes

1   U.S. Department of Health and Human Services, Centers for Disease Control and Prevention, National Center for Health Statistics, "Health, United States, 2007," Library of Congress Catalog no. 76-641496.

2   J. A. Poisal, C. Truffer, S. Smith, A. Sisko, C. Cowan, S. Keehan, and B. Dickensheets, "Health Spending Projections through 2016: Modest Changes Obscure Part D's Impact," Health Aff (Millwood) 26, no. 2 (2007): w242–w253.

3   R. Wyden and B. Bennett, "Finally, Fixing Health Care: What's Different Now?" Health Aff (Millwood) 27, no. 3 (2008): 689–692, http://content.healthaffairs.org.

4   U.S. Department of Health and Human Services, Centers for Disease Control and Prevention, National Center for Health Statistics, "Health, United States, 2007," Library of Congress Catalog no. 76-641496.

5   U.S. Department of Health and Human Services, Centers for Disease Control and Prevention, National Center for Health Statistics, "Health, United States, 2007," Library of Congress Catalog no. 76-641496.

6   Kaiser Family Foundation, Kaiser Commission on Medicaid and the Uninsured, "Health Insurance Coverage in America, 2005 Data Update," May 2007.

7   Kaiser Family Foundation and Health Research and Educational Trust, "Employer Health Benefits, 2007 Summary of Findings," http://www.health08.org.

8   U.S. Department of Health and Human Services, Centers for Disease Control and Prevention, National Center for Health Statistics, "Health, United States, 2007," Library of Congress Catalog no. 76-641496. "Expenditures for Health Services and Supplies and Percent Distribution, by Type of Payer: United States, Selected Years 1987–2005." Data compiled by Centers for Medicare and Medicaid Services.

9   Health Policy Program, New America Foundation, "Employer Health
     Costs in a Global Economy: A Competitive Disadvantage for U.S. Firms,"
     May 2008, http://newamerica.net.

10   Health Policy Program, New America Foundation, "Employer Health
     Costs in a Global Economy: A Competitive Disadvantage for U.S. Firms,"
     May 2008, http://newamerica.net.

11   Excerpt from Queen Elizabeth's Christmas message, Dec. 25, 1999,
     http://www.winstonchurchill.org/i4a/pages/index.cfm?pageid=817.

12   *The New York Times Magazine*, "Compulsory Insurance Help to Medical
     Sciences," December 3, 1916, http://query.nytimes.com.

13   Melissa Thomasson, "Health Insurance in the United States," EH.Net
     Encyclopedia, edited by Robert Whaples, April 18, 2003, http://eh.net/
     encyclopedia/article/thomasson.insurance.health.us.

14   David Blumenthal, "Employer-Sponsored Health Insurance in the United
     States—Origins and Implications," New Eng J of Med 355 (July 6, 2006):
     82–88.

15   M. A. Thomasson, "From Sickness to Health: The Twentieth Century
     Development of U.S. Health Insurance," Explor Econ Hist 39 (2002):
     233–253.

16   M. A. Thomasson, "From Sickness to Health: The Twentieth Century
     Development of U.S. Health Insurance," Explor Econ Hist 39 (2002):
     233–253.

17   Social Security Online, Social Security History, "Medicare Is Signed into
     Law," http://www.ssa.gov/history/lbjsm.html.

18   J. Gabel, S. DiCarlo, C. Sullivan, and T. Rice, "Employer-Sponsored Health
     Insurance, 1989," DataWatch Health Affairs (Fall 1990): 161–175.

19   P. Starr, *The Social Transformation of American Medicine* (New York: Basic
     Books, 1982).

20   *The New York Times Magazine*, "Compulsory Insurance Help to Medical
     Sciences," December 3, 1916, http://query.nytimes.com.

CHAPTER 2

THE BUSINESS OF MANAGING BENEFITS

"Health is the greatest gift, contentment the greatest wealth, faithfulness the best relationship."

—Buddha

Employers are being squeezed from nearly every angle when it comes to managing their health-care costs. Since 2000, health-care spending has been increasing at two to five times the rate of inflation.[1] Factors that will continue to drive health-care costs in the future include more treatment of chronic health problems, increased spending for advances in health-care technology, higher prescription drug costs, and an aging population.

While employers have anxiously watched as their health insurance premiums increased nearly 100 percent since 2000,[2] employees have also had to keep digging deeper to pay their share as the average increase continues to race ahead of their earnings and inflation. In 2007, employees paid an average annual premium of almost $4,500 for single coverage and more than $12,000 for family coverage.[3]

Over the years, employers have tried a number of approaches for managing the rising costs of health care. The efforts that focused strictly on trying to rein in the cost of health care often meant sacrificing the quality of the care employees received. Efforts aimed at improving quality of care added to health-care costs, and access has always been an issue.

For employers, their cost-cutting attempts have been like playing a game of chance with little insight into the odds. The cards have been stacked against them from the beginning. In the interest of saving money, how many more health benefits can be cut and how much more quality can be compromised before the house of cards comes crashing down?

Cost-Cutting Measures Often Cut Corners

Beginning in the late 1980s, companies initially focused on curbing rising health-care costs by reducing benefits and shifting more of the cost burden to employees. Employers latched onto the idea of managed care because it provided a way to hold the line on rising costs by reducing payments to network providers and limiting access to higher-priced specialty care.

Managed-care plans, such as health maintenance organizations (HMOs) and preferred provider organizations (PPOs), soon became the option of choice that employers offered their employees. Fee-for-service plans became a thing of the past. At one time, up to 95 percent of employees with company-sponsored health benefits were enrolled in some kind of managed-care plan.[4]

However, as managed-care costs began to climb, the monthly contribution required of employees increased, as did the annual plan deductibles. Even though managed care was considered *the* answer to keeping health-care costs in check, many were concerned that the tight controls resulted in a lack of the quality of care. A growing backlash from unhappy consumers resulted in many states enacting legislation to address their complaints about issues such as maternity length of stay, emergency care coverage, and patient rights.

But quality wasn't the only issue on consumers' minds. Many employees were reluctant to accept more out-of-pocket expenses to co-payments and increasingly higher deductibles. At most companies, employees weren't able to express their frustration to their employers in a meaningful way—but union workers were able to demonstrate their opposition to cost shifting in large numbers.

In January 2003, about 20,000 General Electric Company (GE) workers launched a national strike against their employer to protest higher co-pays for their Health Care Preferred medical plan. The strike was held before contract negotiations began and lasted two days; it focused the country's attention on how corporations were shifting costs to employees as a way to cope with rising health-care costs.

Also in 2003, members of the Communications Workers of America and the International Brotherhood of Electrical Workers stalled contract negotiations with Verizon to protest the shifting of health-care costs onto current and retired employees. Companies such as Safeway and General Motors also faced strong union resistance to their attempts at shifting the rising health-care costs to their employees.

However, not all costs are shifted to workers; some companies pass their health-care costs onto their customers. For example, the cost of providing health-care benefits to Ford Motor Company employees adds about $1,200 to every Ford car and truck built in the United States.[5]

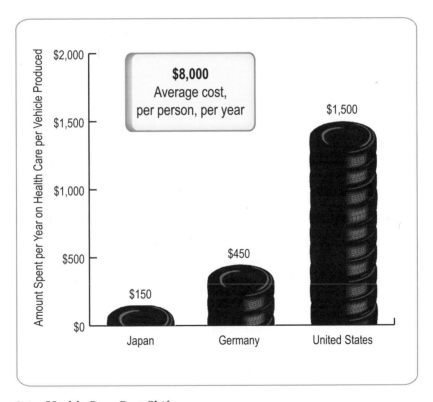

2.1   Health-Care-Cost Shift

The most extreme form of cost shifting is simply eliminating health-care coverage as an employee benefit. This option seems inevitable for businesses that are unable to manage annual premium increases as a cost of doing business, which is especially true for small businesses. The 9-percent decline in employer-sponsored health benefits from 2000 to 2007 was the result of companies with 3–199 employees dropping their health-care coverage.[6] In businesses with 3–9 workers, the rate of companies offering health benefits dropped 12 percent, from 57 to 45 percent, during that same time period.[7]

These statistics represent millions of hardworking Americans who must make the decision to forgo health insurance completely, find insurance on their own, or seek out employment with a company that still offers a health insurance benefit.

From Cutting Costs to Improving Quality

Some efforts at cost shifting may have worked to contain costs in the short term, but they weren't effective for driving any meaningful change in health-care costs for the long term or for improving the quality of the care. Employers had a difficult time managing the business of benefits because they underestimated the power that providers had in terms of autonomy and their ability to control health-care costs. Employers also didn't have the depth of detailed information they needed to gain purchasing power, and the information they did have came from those with vested interests: their insurance carriers and other vendors.

Employers learned the hard way that cost shifting was not a sustainable business model for financing health-care benefits. So instead of shifting costs, employers shifted their thinking. If costs were to be contained, employees would have to share more of the responsibility of their health care and the associated costs. Employers began offering high-deductible health plans, some of which were offered with a savings account meant to help pay for out-of-pocket expenses not covered by the plan. These health savings plans are part of a group of health insurance plans known as consumer-directed health care (CDHC). These plans transform employees from passive health-care users to active health-care consumers.

Consumer-directed plans are sometimes referred to as high-deductible health plans with a savings option (HDHP/SO), and many also offer a tiered-benefit design to give employees choices based on their health-care needs. These plans can empower employees to better spend the money allocated to them, as long as they have the comparative information about the cost and quality of health-care providers and specific services. Three kinds of consumer-directed plans include medical savings accounts, health savings accounts, and health reimbursement accounts.

Medical savings accounts (MSAs) were the first wave of consumer-directed plans created in the late 1990s. These accounts consisted of a portable tax-exempt pool of money that employers and employees could contribute to, up to a set amount. MSAs were typically available to firms of 50 and fewer employees or the self-employed.

Health savings accounts (HSAs) are another kind of consumer-directed plan, created by the Medicare Modernization Act of 2003. HSAs are like tax-free retirement accounts, where the accounts are held to cover qualified medical expenses.

The fundamental flaw in this concept is that employers aren't able to budget for the unknown. The anticipated expenses of what an employer might spend are based on such high numbers that there's the risk of not putting enough money in and then having that money either be exhausted quickly or not be used appropriately. Employers' abilities to apportion resources correctly require an understanding of the cost, utilization, and risk of their employee population so they can put a sufficient amount into the account.

Health reimbursement accounts (HRAs) are IRS-sanctioned arrangements that are funded by the employer. HRAs are more flexible than HSAs, and many provide tax-free funds for employees to use for health-care-related expenses, either in addition to or instead of health insurance benefits. HRAs are usually associated with high-deductible health plans.

An important aspect of CDHPs is the tiered programs that employers provide. Tiered plans allow consumers to select from different levels of co-pays and deductibles. These tiers are a form of incentive or financial reward for employees and are designed to guide them toward certain providers, programs, or other avenues to encourage them to better manage their own care. Tiered programs encourage employees to take advantage of less costly options such as using generic medications as opposed to brand-name drugs or visiting certain providers that are deemed to provide higher-quality care.

The downside to tiered programs is that because they are based on cost, they may have a negative impact on employees or their dependents who suffer with chronic disease, especially in terms of driving them to the right options.

Creating Proactive Health-Care Consumers

Consumer-directed health-care plans can help engage employees in making more cost-effective and quality-conscious health-care choices, but they need the right tools to be able to do so. Employers wanting to implement consumer-directed plans need to provide employees with the right health-care decision-making tools. This may sound simple, but currently, the level of transparency is such that consumers don't have access to all of the metrics or quantitative measures of the health care they are consuming. They need basic comparison information, such as the cost of providers' services, to help them make intelligent health-care decisions.

However, because health care has become so complicated, this information isn't always available in a form that consumers can comprehend. The challenge of consumer-directed plans is similar to sending a college freshman to the campus library on the first day of school and saying, "Here's all the information you need to learn whatever you want; just choose the books." Without a structured curriculum, that student wouldn't know where to start or even the most important questions to ask. To be most effective, consumer-directed plans need to deliver more personalized information in a manner that engages consumers by giving them transparency in making choices.

Another issue surrounding CDHPs is whether they will have the desired effect on containing health-care costs. Many employers are still evaluating the effectiveness of the design of these programs. One problem is that consumer-directed health plans weren't designed for individuals with chronic illnesses, such as complicated diabetes or congestive heart failure. Because these health-care consumers require ongoing care, they may reach their deductible limits quickly, increasing their out-of-pocket costs. Some may even choose to forgo necessary care.

Prevention Strategies Offer Additional Benefits

Consumer-driven health plans can benefit from the addition of two components: pay-for-performance initiatives and disease management. These interventions are designed to affect both the cost and the quality of care.

Pay for performance, also called P4P or value-based purchasing, is a system of financial rewards for health-care providers and facilities that meet predetermined quality performance measures. Medicare has P4P initiatives in place to encourage improved quality of care to its beneficiaries for reducing health-care costs and improving the quality of care, from physicians' offices to nursing homes and dialysis facilities.

In the corporate world, companies work with their insurers to reward providers who offer better-quality care at a lower cost. Some P4P programs reward physicians who effectively treat individuals with chronic and high-cost health conditions, including diabetes, congestive heart failure, and chronic obstructive pulmonary disease. Programs also address costly mental health issues such as depression.

Most P4P programs include certain outcome measures, and physicians receive a financial reward for meeting them. However, quality is difficult to measure without any consistent measures of how it is defined in terms of outcomes. As an example, one measure for physicians is tracking the hemoglobin A1c level of all of their patients with diabetes. This blood test is a measure of the overall effectiveness of blood glucose control over a period of time. The outcome measure is reaching a certain A1c level.

But what is an adequately controlled hemoglobin A1c level for a diabetic? What is acceptable in terms of control? What is acceptable in terms of progression of diabetic retinopathy when somebody needs laser treatment? Because these measures of quality are ambiguous, creating consistent measures of performance becomes difficult.

Pay for Performance or Pay for Productivity?

A key question about the pay-for-performance approach is whether it compensates doctors with the right financial incentives for the right quality measures. Performance is only one measure, and it shouldn't be limited to clinical outcomes. From a physician's perspective, "pay for performance" should really be "pay for productivity." Productivity should be the end point for success as opposed to a measure of clinical control.

When I was practicing as an ophthalmologist, I would examine patients for glaucoma. The outcome for glaucoma typically is measured by whether the pressure in the eye is controlled. Control in this case means that the optic nerve has no further damage that can be measured directly by looking at the surface of the eye for loss of nerve fibers and/or indirect measures of visual field loss that are quantified by a computer. As a clinician, I had objective metrics to measure whether the condition was progressing. But *never* was I treating the patient with the outcome of whether this individual with glaucoma was functioning productively at work as opposed to a clinical measure.

Productivity can be measured by the number of lost days from work as a result of the glaucoma or other chronic illness. Productivity can also be measured by the output, such as how many widgets are manufactured in a day. But not every industry is measured by widgets, and productivity measures can be especially ambiguous.

However, direct health-care costs account for only a quarter of the total cost of chronic diseases such as pulmonary conditions, hypertension, heart disease, diabetes, and arthritis.[8] Chronic conditions account for more than 75 cents of every dollar spent on health care and represent $1 trillion a year in lost productivity.[9] Absenteeism is measured as lost time from work, but presenteeism also costs when employees aren't productive at work because of their chronic conditions.

Pay for productivity would consider the direct and indirect costs of an individual with an illness, not just the cost of treating the illness itself. Pay for productivity is an important measure of health care and should be considered as a viable alternative to the pay-for-performance model.

Disease Management Programs Are a Promising Approach

Disease management is an intervention approach designed to help employers manage the cost of health care by better managing the conditions that consume the majority of the resources. Employers who offer disease management programs to their employees purchase disease management services from companies that specialize in this option. Employees or their family members with chronic conditions receive special health-care services to help them manage their illnesses. As with pay-for-performance programs, with participation come certain financial incentives.

The Partnership to Fight Chronic disease advocates for workplace approaches such as prevention, wellness, and disease management programs to help stem rising health-care costs. Disease management programs include diabetes prevention programs, weight loss programs for the morbidly obese, and smoking cessation programs. From my experience working with employers during the past eight years, about 90 percent of a company's health benefit cost is driven by 10–15 percent of the population. The conditions driving the preponderance of costs include diabetes, cardiovascular diseases such as hypertension and pulmonary conditions, and low-back pain. However, the bulk of the costs is being driven not by the individual with one condition but by individuals with one condition and also a complication of that condition, called comorbidity.

Disease management programs offer promising results, but they're not the silver bullet in terms of solving the problems of health-care cost and quality. Employers simply don't have enough information on the risks and comorbidities of the employee population. Risk includes all of the factors that might affect certain employee populations. Risk information helps employers budget for health-care-cost increases and declines in productivity that may result from these conditions in the future.

Disease management vendors, or the insurance carriers providing disease management services, are responsible for providing employers with information about the return on their investments. But this information is based on the metrics of success they provide. Employers must be able to independently evaluate the value of these programs.

Health-Care Coalitions Influence Cost and Quality

The old adage "misery loves company" may apply to employers frustrated with managing their health-care-benefits programs. In the mid-1990s, when they got tired of fighting the health-care-financing battle on their own, they began to form purchasing groups. The movement started with employers in cities and regions across the country, and national coalitions soon followed. With a "strength in numbers" mindset, coalitions banded together to find ways to optimize their health-care investment. The goal was to leverage their resources as a group to provide higher-quality medical services at a better price. Working together, they could negotiate discounts on products and services, form physician networks, reduce pharmacy costs, and gain new reporting tools and benchmark analyses.

Examples of these coalitions include the National Business Coalition on Health, a nonprofit membership group of about 60 employer-based health-care coalitions from across the country. In 2008, its membership represented 10,000 employers and 34 million employees and their dependents.[10] An example of an individual health-care-purchasing coalition is the Buyers Health Care Action Group in Minnesota. In June 2008, the group launched a pay-for-performance pilot program for physicians treating patients suffering from depression.

Another example of an effective coalition is the Leapfrog Group, based in Washington, D.C. The group was formed in 2000 and has worked to advance the cause of improved patient safety and higher-quality health care. The group's employee members work to increase transparency and access to health-care information by annually asking hospitals to voluntarily complete a hospital quality and safety survey. The results are shared with consumers to help them make informed health-care decisions.

Employer groups such as these recognize the need for initiatives that help increase transparency for health-care consumers. Transparency here means that each group is able to base its decisions on cost, utilization, and risk as pertaining to consumption of health-care services among each employer's population.

Strength in Numbers:
The Alliance for Wellness ROI Inc.

The Alliance for Wellness ROI Inc. is a nonprofit, intercompany cooperative focused on demonstrating the value of corporate wellness programs. The alliance's activities are directed at showing how a company's preventive health program can be objectively measured to determine the return on its investment. The alliance would not have become a reality if it weren't for one person's firsthand experience dealing with the rising costs of health care.

As a manager of health and welfare plans with Schlumberger, Lillian Petty was frustrated by the ineffectiveness of the company's ongoing efforts to control health-care costs. Through effective plan management, including constant review and manipulation of the plan design to encourage cost-effective care, coupled with various preventive-care measures, Schlumberger was able to consistently beat health-care trend by about half. Despite these ongoing efforts, health-care costs were still increasing at a pace greater than inflation.

Instead of waiting for the government to take action, Petty took the challenge to the people who paid the bills—the employers. She invited some of her colleagues at the Council on Employee Benefits to explore the ways that they could work together to manage health-care costs and improve their own populations' health.

Target: Population Health

In 2000, Petty recommended and implemented an integrated approach to managing health and wellness at Schlumberger in partnership with the company's quality, safety, and health group and the business operating group. Because the company believed that prevention was as important as managing disease, Schlumberger was willing to invest in the effort and support employees in managing their health care.

To measure the effectiveness of the company's wellness initiatives, Petty worked with Schlumberger's finance team and the International Medical Advisory Board of EHE, a company with a long history in the health and wellness field. Schlumberger was

continues ▶

seeing positive results on its investment in prevention, and Petty wanted to share that information with other companies.

In October 2004, she held a meeting for companies interested in joining the alliance, and four decided to participate: BMW of North America, Henry Ford Health System, Kraft Foods Global Inc., and MasterCard Worldwide. These companies joined Schlumberger as the founding members of the Alliance for Wellness ROI. They shared information about their wellness programs' successes and challenges and worked together to aggregate the information to produce a return-on-investment methodology that could become a standard.

The group began by defining all of the components of a wellness program, ranging from disease management and fitness programs to smoking cessation and health risk appraisals. The next step was measuring participation rates, which turned out to be trickier because people tended to migrate between programs on the basis of their changing needs.

The survey showed that the top-five health conditions were similar across all five companies. Even though each was in a different business, the participants were representative of the nation's health-care problems, with cancer, diabetes, and obesity in the top three. In addition, the survey showed that each company was spending between $2 and $5 per member per month on wellness programs, but none of the companies had a way to track the returns on those investments.

During the survey process, the group tapped into the expertise of epidemiologists from Columbia University and actuaries from Touchstone Consulting Group to validate the alliance's methodology and help establish meaningful benchmarks.

The Alliance Is Formed

In 2005, the Alliance for Wellness ROI was formed with the goal for creating a standard modeling methodology as a resource to help companies make decisions regarding their health and wellness programs. The alliance's three specific areas of focus included the following:

1. Conduct an annual survey to develop a clear definition of the components of successful wellness programs.

2. Build an integrated return-on-investment model that produces a valuation report of expected ROI each year.

3. Build a data repository by using a technology partner to automate the collection and aggregation of data to produce useable information.

The alliance understands the importance of demonstrating the value of corporate wellness programs to organizations and their employees as well. The first round of ROI analysis, conducted by Touchstone Consulting, was based on approximately three to four years' worth of data. It showed that individual company ROIs ranged from $0.40 to $2.54 saved for every $1.00 spent on a wellness program. Other interesting findings from the analysis concluded that disease management and nurse hotline programs had the greatest impact on reducing health-care claims in the short term; preventive-care and employee assistance programs had a much smaller impact on reducing health-care costs over the same period.

continues ▶

Additionally, through the use of health risk appraisal data, Touchstone discovered the following:

- Medical and drug claims increase as an individual's body mass index (BMI) increases, most notably at BMI levels in excess of 35.

- Tobacco users consistently incur more health-care costs than non–tobacco users.

- Health-care costs and overall cholesterol levels are not correlated.

Next Steps for the Alliance

After four years of working as a cooperative group, the alliance now has individual financial measures and an aggregate measure of the pool group of data. Other companies will soon be asked to join the alliance's efforts to implement an integrated ROI measurement, a data repository, and an annual benchmark program.

Even though Petty understands that wellness programs can't make every participant healthy, the alliance will have a standardized and reputable way to help companies manage their health-care costs. This is especially important for large companies that still provide health-care benefits to their retiree populations. The alliance's efforts will help benefits managers across the country decide what kinds of wellness programs they need to implement and will aid them in building a solid business case to predict return on investment.

The Other Side of Consumer-Directed Health Plans

Proponents of CDHPs tout the ability of these plans to lower health-care costs, but there is some debate about the source of these savings. It is still not clear whether the plans are actually saving money or whether the savings come from adverse selection bias. While younger, healthier employees are disproportionately attracted to CDHPs, less healthy employees select traditional insurance plans, causing premiums for those plans to rise. Because an employer bases its risk on a majority of healthy employees who won't use much of their allocated health-care dollars, the amount available declines for the individuals with chronic conditions who are most likely to use the funds.

Vendor-Independent Reporting Can Drive Change

Despite all of these attempts to hold down costs, employers still haven't hit on the right formula. The key issue is that most employers still do not have all of the information to control health-care costs. Employers may not have the appropriate cost, utilization, and risk metrics, or maybe they don't have access to the right metrics or don't have the infrastructure and technology to give them the required level of transparency into those metrics. Employers simply don't have vendor-independent reporting, and that is what undermines their ability to drive efficiencies.

Employers are at a distinct disadvantage when negotiating with providers, whether individually or in group-purchasing coalitions, because the providers have more information about their employee populations than they do. They are dependent on vendors to provide them with the information they need in order to make sound health-care-benefits decisions. Consider what would happen in the automotive manufacturing marketplace if Ford Motor Company had to ask Bridgestone what kind of tires it should buy.

Vendor-independent reporting gives employers the necessary clout in order to drive change, and it's the first step in health-care empowerment for them—and their employees. Empowered health-care consumers will have more options for how they finance and manage their care. Market-based models ultimately help consumers because a competitive marketplace helps drive down cost and improve quality.

No matter which approach employers take to managing their health-care benefits, they need to have certain components in place. These include the infrastructure and technology to give comprehensive health-care information. They need to have the right metrics of cost, utilization, and risk to understand the real health-care costs. In addition, while there's been a push for adopting technology to get more health information to consumers, there's a lack of consistent standards in reporting those data. This is yet another prerequisite for managing the economics of health care.

Chapter 2—Key Messages

- Employers have tried many approaches to managing their escalating health-care costs, from shifting costs to employees to sharing the cost with them. However, some of the initiatives that helped lower health-care costs jeopardized the quality of care.

- Small businesses are especially vulnerable to increases in health-care premiums, and some find it necessary to eliminate health-care coverage completely in order to remain in business.

- Consumer-directed health plans require employees to become more proactive health-care consumers; however, consumerism depends on access to good information and the availability of good health information tools.

- Pay-for-performance and disease management programs are two interventions aimed at lowering health-care costs and improving quality, but measuring their effectiveness has been difficult.

- Pay for productivity is a more accurate measure because it includes the direct and indirect costs of an individual with an illness.

- Health-care coalitions have strength in numbers of employers, but they also need more transparency to make better purchasing decisions.

- The key to empowering health-care consumers—both employers and employees—is vendor-independent reporting providing access to the real metrics of cost, utilization, and risk. With the right health information tools, employees can make more informed health-care choices.

Chapter 2—Endnotes

1   National Coalition on Health Care, "Economic Cost Fact Sheet: The Impact of Rising Health Care Costs on the Economy," 2008, http://www.nchc.org/facts/economic/shtml.

2   National Coalition on Health Care, "Economic Cost Fact Sheet: The Impact of Rising Health Care Costs on the Economy," 2008, http://www.nchc.org/facts/economic/shtml.

3   Kaiser Family Foundation and Health Research and Educational Trust, "Employer Health Benefits, 2007 Summary of Findings," http://www.health08.org.

4   J Gabel et al., "Health Benefits in 2004: Four Years of Double-Digit Premium Increases Take Their Toll on Coverage," Health Affairs 23, no. 5 (Sept.–Oct. 2004): 200–209.

5   "About Ford: Our Health Care Policy," http://www.ford.com.

6   Kaiser Family Foundation and Health Research and Educational Trust, "Employer Health Benefits, 2007 Summary of Findings," http://www.health08.org.

7   Kaiser Family Foundation and Health Research and Educational Trust, "Employer Health Benefits, 2007 Summary of Findings," http://www.health08.org.

8   Partnership to Fight Chronic Disease, *Almanac of Chronic Disease*, 2008 ed., http://www.fightchronicdisease.org.

9   Partnership to Fight Chronic Disease, *Almanac of Chronic Disease*, 2008 ed., http://www.fightchronicdisease.org.

10   National Business Coalition on Health, "About NBCH," http://www.nbch.org.

CHAPTER 3

THE BALANCING ACT

"We must turn to nature itself, to the observations of the body in health and in disease to learn the truth."

—Hippocrates

For many years, health-care benefits weren't considered an important part of the business equation. Instead of being regarded as a cost center, benefits were part of the reciprocal contract that companies forged with one of their important constituencies, their employees. Employees invest their time, skills, and talent in a company to help make it profitable, and they expect to receive a good return on their investment in the form of monetary compensation and health-care benefits. Companies also have a reciprocal arrangement with another important constituent, their shareholders. Shareholders expect a return on their investment by being associated with a company that's profitable and competitive in the marketplace.

Because companies can't survive without either employees or shareholders, they need to continuously balance both sets of constituent expectations to keep each group investing in the company. Is it possible to meet each group's expectations when it comes to balancing financial risk versus health risk? Shareholders expect reduced

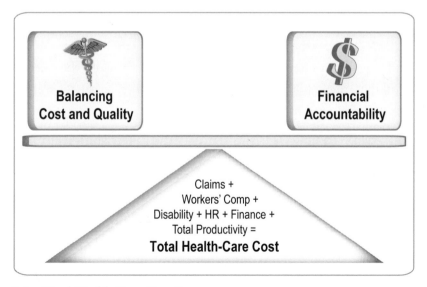

3.1   Total Health-Care-Cost Seesaw

health-care costs to result in a healthier bottom line; employees expect greater value from their health-care dollars. Employers are caught somewhere in the middle, wondering how far they can push the envelope in terms of optimizing the cost versus the quality of the health benefits.

With shareholders on one end of the seesaw and employees on the other, what can companies do to assure that neither side is up when the other is down? If health-care costs can be controlled, who will end up at the top of the seesaw? Is it possible to have more than one winner? A balancing act like this requires an in-depth understanding of health-care financing in order to find the perfect equilibrium.

When CFOs Became Involved

By now, we're all too familiar with the double-digit increases in health insurance premiums that companies began to experience in early 2000. It's difficult to believe now, but in the mid-1990s, health-care inflation was only 4.8 percent.[1] The 11-percent premium increase in the spring of 2000–2001 was the largest increase since the early 1990s,[2] and it certainly caught the attention of chief financial officers across the country. Until that time, most companies absorbed health-care-benefit costs by growing revenue in an increasingly robust economy.

However, a series of events combined to form a perfect storm that would forever change the way CFOs thought about health care. Beginning in early 2000, the tech stock bubble burst and deleted $5 trillion in paper wealth from the NASDAQ.[3] Companies were hit with compromised revenues at the same time that health-care costs began rising. Had the dot-com bubble not burst, companies may have been able to absorb the effects of rising health-care costs, but that's when they were hit the hardest.

The CFO's Patellar Reflex

Prior to the confluence of these major events, employee health benefits were a responsibility of the human resources department and were considered a necessary part of recruiting and retaining employees. Once companies started feeling the pain associated with rising benefits costs, the approach changed. C-level executives stepped in to try to stop the bleeding, and their knee-jerk reaction was to shift the cost of health care onto employees. We now know what happened when costs were pushed onto union workers: unions pushed back.

Seemingly overnight, health benefits moved from a value-added benefit to a cost center, which meant that CFOs had to quickly gain an understanding of health benefits financing and its impact on the bottom line. However, the complexity of how employee health coverage is structured at most companies presents barriers to CFOs who need a clear view of benefit costs and internal controls. The health-care-spending metrics that companies were receiving from their insurance carriers, vendors, pharmacy benefits managers, and disease management companies didn't provide the depth of information CFOs needed to adapt to a changing benefits landscape.

In order for CFOs to be able to make effective decisions regarding health benefits, they need to gain visibility into the total cost of the company's health care, and that information needs to be accessed in a timely manner. The saying "time is money" takes on an added urgency when the inflation rate is on the rise; the longer it takes to get visibility, the more it costs the company. The five key operational challenges impeding CFOs' ability to manage health benefits include the following:

1. No timely access to integrated financial, human resources, and clinical health benefits information. Information is difficult to access because of the number of vendors and systems that are in place. In addition, most companies lack the capability to quickly access data from human resources and to integrate that data within finance so they can track vendor performance—yet this capability could help them reduce redundancy and enhance communication across the supply chain.

2. Setbacks in integration schedules. An integrated view to show all metrics impacting health benefit costs across business areas and vendors is needed to reduce the dependence on vendors to provide the information.

3. Lags in financial reporting. Limited benefits and finance integration force human resources and finance to work from different sets of assumptions and even objectives. Increased visibility can be achieved by linking the entire benefits purchase-to-pay cycle, resulting in improved forecasting, budgeting, and financial reporting.

4. Delays in gaining the depth of knowledge and expertise required to use the information. Measuring the total cost and risk of the population can increase the return on investment of benefits strategies and improve the ability to make more timely decisions by quantifying the total costs, both direct and indirect, of individuals' health.

5. Delays and other difficulties in managing and measuring vendor performance. Measuring vendor performance helps to identify savings opportunities and creates greater leverage in contract negotiations.

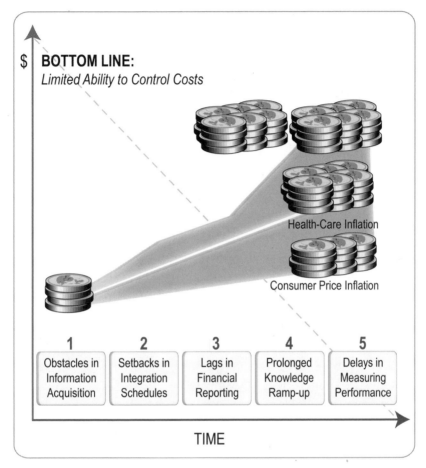

3.2 Five Obstacles to Managing Health Benefits

The magnitude of the problem became more acute in 2004, when McKinsey Quarterly released its research showing that the average Fortune 500 Company could be spending as much on health benefits as it earned in profits in only four short years.[4] Maintaining sustainability became a real issue. The pressure was on for CFOs to find the answer to two key questions: "How are we going to be able to meet shareholder expectations regarding our future health-care liability, and how are we going to pay for it?"

Shareholder Expectations and the Total Health-Care-Cost Equation

When it comes to their health-care benefits, employers are struggling to balance the cost and quality of health benefits with financial accountability. But the benefits supply chain is too complex to provide visibility into all the metrics needed to do this. The supply chain comprises many disparate entities, including plan administrators, physicians, hospitals, specialty providers, consultants, plan enrollees, and internal systems such as the finance and benefits function of the plan sponsor itself. With a supply chain as large and complex as this, it's easy to understand why there is little information transparency and why it makes it difficult for companies to effectively manage their total health-care spending. Accurately forecasting health benefits becomes a difficult if not impossible task.

To give shareholders transparency and visibility in how health benefits will be paid requires a better understanding of the problem. One approach focuses on the specific metrics around incidence of conditions and number of encounters. But this doesn't provide the depth of detail needed to balance the cost and quality of health benefits with financial accountability. Before CFOs can estimate the total health-care cost, they need to have visibility into the total health-care-cost equation.

Claims + Workers' Comp + Disability + HR + Finance + Total Productivity = Total Health Care Cost

The total health-care-cost equation includes the amount spent on medical care paid to those who provide the care, workers' compensation costs, disability costs, health-care premiums, administrative costs, and lost time from work. This equation is different from calculating the cost of health-care spending because it includes the total cost of individuals with an illness as opposed to the cost of the illness alone.

Approximately 40–50 percent of health-care costs are attributable only to the direct costs; the remaining 50–60 percent of costs is attributable to the indirect costs of lost time from work, disability, and productivity. CFOs need to know both direct and indirect health-care costs to understand the total health-care equation.

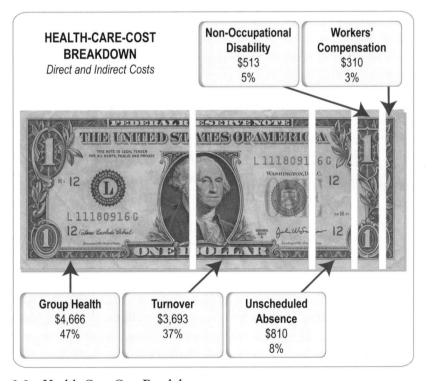

3.3   Health-Care-Cost Breakdown

Consider this example. A defense contractor was spending nearly $1 billion a year on health-care costs. A disease management program was implemented to help manage the costs associated with the contractor's population of workers diagnosed with cardiovascular disease. The amount of health-care spending, the direct cost, was about $24 million. However, when the contractor factored in the indirect costs of lost time from work and disability as they pertained to those individuals with cardiovascular disease, the total health-care cost was almost $78 million—a difference of $54 million.

Adding to the complexity, health-care benefits have been viewed as identical across industries. Because health-care costs differ by industry segment, the financial risk of manufacturing companies is different from that of retail stores. For example, in high tech or manufacturing, margins are closer to 4 or 5 percent, as opposed to retail, where they are about 2 percent. When margins are so low and the trend in health-care benefits is so high, it's difficult for CFOs to understand the financial risk of the company's impending benefit and what impact that will have on business.

That's been the fundamental challenge for companies wanting to meet shareholder expectations. Shareholders want to know what the future liability will be and what impact it will have on corporate performance. CFOs need to use the total health-care equation to determine the liability or they won't be able to meet shareholder expectations.

The Health-Care-Funding Process Is Complicated

Where does the money come from to pay for health-care benefits? Many companies, including most small businesses, rely on commercial insurers to provide their health insurance coverage, but most large companies self-insure. This means that they operate their own insurance plan, through a third-party administrator, to fund their employees' health-care costs.

Few companies have a comprehensive view of how their health benefits are paid, and for most self-insured companies, it's hard to get a handle on how the dollars flow between key players in the supply chain.

At the beginning of the fiscal year, companies set aside health benefits money in a reserve fund. The amount is estimated with the use of actuarial tables and estimates of the expected health-care costs for the year provided by insurance carriers or consultants. These estimates are based on the previous year's results, adjusted for inflation, and the health insurance premiums. A company may have to set aside several million dollars, tens of millions of dollars, or, sometimes, hundreds of millions of dollars into a reserve account that is prefunded to pay the carrier for the company's premiums.

The problem with this approach is that the money in this prefunded account is not available for the company to use for any other purpose. Because the health-care-cost estimates are based on the previous year's totals, the measures might not be an accurate reflection of the current year's costs. The result can be a substantial variance in the amount of the reserve. If this amount were invested appropriately instead of remaining in reserve, it might generate significant returns for the company.

To gain a better understanding of the company's actual health-care cost, CFOs must understand the three metrics of cost, utilization, and risk for their employee population. All three metrics are required to complete the total health-care-cost equation and help to answer questions such as:

- How much is the company spending on employees diagnosed with diabetes, cardiovascular disease, or chronic pulmonary conditions?

- What are the underlying conditions that are driving those costs?

- What are the future direct and indirect health-care costs?

47

- To what degree should we hold our vendors accountable for the costs?

- What are the actual costs versus the estimated costs?

Answering the last question, comparing actual and estimated costs, has a significant impact on the amount the company is going to fund, what amount of liability will be reflected on the balance sheet, and what impact that liability will have on the company's profits. Those are important elements for estimating the impact of health risk based on estimated future financial risk and the effect on earnings per share.

The Ultimate Metric for CFOs

The measure of a company's profitability, and the ultimate metric for CFOs, is earnings per share. This is an important performance metric that CFOs and other executives need to report back to shareholders to meet their expectations for understanding the company's health-care liability and how it will be paid. However, few companies have a blueprint for the impact benefits strategies have on corporate performance and how that translates into the impact on earnings per share.

CFOs should use several elements for calculating earnings per share. These include medical and prescription plan designs, workers' compensation, health management of the population, vendor management, enrollment and cost sharing, and forecasting, budgeting, and reporting. These elements are measured by asking the following questions:

- What is the health benefit expense per employee per year?

- What is the health benefit expense as a percentage of payroll?

- What is the health benefit expense as a percentage of net income?

- What is the productivity of the workforce?

- What is the amount of overfunding as a percentage of health benefit expense?

- What are the overcharges as a percent of health benefit expense?

KEY MANAGEMENT LEVERS

- Medical Plan Design
- Workers' Compensation
- Vendor Management
- Forecasting, Budgeting, Reporting
- Rx Plan Design
- Population Health Management
- Cost-Sharing Enrollment

MEASURE AND CONTROL

- Health Benefits Expense Per Employee Per Year
- Health Benefits Expenses as a % of Payroll
- Health Benefits Expenses as a % of Net Income
- Workforce Productivity
- Overfunding as a % of Health Benefits Expense
- Overcharges as a % of Health Benefits Expense

RESULTS

- Operating Margin
- Asset Management
- Corporate Performance

FINANCIAL GOAL
Earnings Per Share

3.4   Impact of Health Benefits on Earnings Per Share

The resulting information provides the three important measures of earnings per share: operating margin, asset management, and corporate performance.

Reporting the Company's Health-Care Liability

Earnings per share is the metric shareholders use to gauge corporate performance, and it is also an important element in reporting the company's health-care liability.

The Sarbanes-Oxley Act of 2002 had a profound effect on employer-sponsored health benefits. The legislation required C-level executives to regularly certify that their financial disclosures were accurate and that controls were in place to assure that material facts were not omitted. However, in recent years, the Securities and Exchange Commission investigated several companies because their liability estimates, from an actuarial standpoint, were intentionally underestimated to under-reflect their liability so that earnings would appear to be more than they were. Companies now have to be more transparent in meeting shareholders' expectations about how health-care liabilities are going to be paid and the impact of those liabilities on earnings per share. This emphasizes the need for creating greater sensitivity in the measurement of future liability because of its impact on earnings.

With the right metrics in place, corporate executives can get more sensitivity and detail on health-care cost, utilization, and risk so that they can better forecast and budget the dollars in the reserve fund. A blueprint for how health benefits affect corporate performance helps all parties understand the impact of the liability on earnings per share.

Retiree Costs Compound the Problem

The issue of costs for retiree health benefits has become a major problem for companies with a large retiree population. The aging of the population, as well as the structure of extremely robust benefits, has increased the retiree liability, or what's referred to as legacy costs. For many companies, this represents a liability that continues to grow as more employees retire and earnings decrease. Calculating these legacy costs also has implications from a financial reporting point. In the past, companies didn't have to account for these costs. However, now they must record costs of funding this liability.

The health benefits that retirees receive in addition to their pension plan are called other postemployment benefits (OPEB) and, depending on the employer, may include medical care, dental care, vision and hearing care prescriptions, long-term disability, and other health-related benefits. OPEB costs were once accounted for on a pay-as-you-go basis during a time when these costs were a few tenths of a percent of payroll. Now, these costs represent 5–10 percent of payroll, and that percentage is increasing every year. In addition, under Sarbanes-Oxley, companies are now required to provide detail, within the context of the balance sheet, on the actual retiree liability instead of listing it as a footnote on the financial statement.

In addition, the health costs of retirees and their dependents can be more expensive because of the overall risk these individuals bear in their health. The challenge for employers, from an economic perspective, is how to estimate the retirees' future risk and the impact of the liability that has to be reported on the balance sheet. This presents a challenge for companies with a large retiree population, such as defense contractors or manufacturing companies.

VISTEON CORPORATION AND SUBSIDIARIES
CONSOLIDATED BALANCE SHEETS
(Dollars in Millions)

	(Unaudited) 30-Sep 2007	31-Dec 2006
ASSETS		
Cash and equivalents	$ 1,422	$ 1,057
Accounts receivable, net	1,289	1,245
Interests in accounts receivable transferred	463	482
Inventories, net	535	520
Other current assets	250	261
Total current assets	**3,959**	**3,565**
Equity in net assets of nonconsolidated affiliates	233	224
Property and equipment, net	2,798	3,034
Other noncurrent assets	**129**	**115**
Total assets	**$ 7,119**	**$ 6,938**
LIABILITIES AND SHAREHOLDERS' DEFICIT		
Short-term debt, including current portion of long-term debt	$ 109	$ 100
Accounts payable	1,781	1,825
Accrued employee liabilities	307	323
Other current liabilities	**336**	**320**
Total current liabilities	**2,533**	**2,568**
Long-term debt	2,604	2,128
Employee benefits, including pensions	641	924
Postretirement benefits other than pensions	629	747
Deferred income taxes	193	170
Other noncurrent liabilities	393	318
Minority interests in consolidated subsidiaries	288	271
Shareholders' deficit		
Preferred stock (par value $1.00, 50 million shares authorized, none outstanding)	—	—
Common stock (par value $1.00, 500 million shares authorized, 131 million shares issued, 130 million and 129 million shares outstanding, respectively)	131	131
Stock warrants	127	127
Additional paid-in capital	3,405	3,398
Accumulated deficit	(3,973)	(3,606)
Accumulated other comprehensive income (loss)	160	(216)
Other	(12)	(22)
Total shareholders' deficit	**(162)**	**(188)**
Total liabilities and shareholders' deficit	**$ 7,119**	**$ 6,938**

3.5   Sample Balance Sheet

The Financial Accounting Standards Board (FASB) has implemented new pension accounting standards, and companies are now required to report the funded status of their pension and OPEB plans on their balance sheet. This will bring transparency to pension accounting by assuring that the real economic liability of pension plans is reflected properly on the balance sheet.

Moving Retiree Benefits off of the Balance Sheet

Many companies have eliminated their retiree medical benefits as one way of moving the cost of health care off of their balance sheets. However, others have shifted their retiree health-care liabilities to voluntary employee benefit associations (VEBAs), trusts that hold the funds to pay for health benefits. Taking the retiree liabilities off of balance sheets can transfer billions in retiree health obligations into a VEBA. This improves the financial outlook for companies and also helps protect retiree medical benefits. The VEBA assumes the financial risk of managing the plan and its assets. VEBAs are funded by employer contributions, employee contributions, or both and can be funded over time. In exchange for providing retirees with a health benefit, the defined contribution offers cost predictability for employers.

In 2006, Goodyear Tire and the USW were able to use a VEBA to reach a strike-ending agreement. In this instance, Goodyear transferred more than $1 billion in health-care liability for retirees and made a one-time payment into the VEBA. In 2007, several unions, including the UAW and the Steelworkers unions, were able to negotiate VEBAs for their retirees at General Motors and Chrysler. The key element to the agreement was that GM could remove the value of its future retiree health benefits from its balance sheet.

Small Businesses Have Bigger Problems

Small businesses are at a disadvantage when it comes to health-care benefits. Unlike big companies that self-insure, small businesses purchase their health plans from commercial insurers or managed-care companies. Because of their size, small businesses have little bargaining power when negotiating their benefits packages. In addition, because of the smaller size of the employee population, small businesses have to cope with the concept of adverse selection.

Adverse selection causes health-care costs to rise because a larger number of individuals with health conditions enroll in the employer's plan while healthier individuals opt out of employer-sponsored health insurance. What happens over time is that those who are relatively unhealthy end up staying with their employer because they are covered by insurance. Healthier employees who don't use as many health benefits tend not to be as enticed by health care to stay with the company.

This means that smaller firms find it more difficult to offer health insurance because their risk pool is getting more expensive. Research shows that an increasing number of small businesses are choosing not to offer health benefits because of the cost.

Managing Employee Expectations— The Other Side of the Seesaw

Employer-sponsored health care has been an important part of how companies do business for so many years that it seems like an entitlement. Employers managing the employee side of the seesaw are trying to balance the employees' expectations for a high-quality health benefits program while attempting to optimize health-care costs. We've seen the previous efforts by employers from cost shifting to cost sharing.

With consumer-directed plans, employers have tried to address the issue of health-care cost by empowering employees to take on more responsibility for choosing the benefits or programs that best meet their needs. But the problem with this approach is that employees don't have enough information about their benefits to estimate how much money they may have to spend in the future on the basis of their risk, and they don't know how to access that information. Employers haven't been able to provide meaningful information to their employees regarding cost, utilization, and risk. This has been a major gap in managing employees' expectations.

Employees are already knowledgeable consumers in other areas of the marketplace. As consumers, they can easily search the Internet to find and compare prices on goods and services from books to cars, from carpet cleaning to locating real estate investments overseas. However, it's curious that more information is available for comparing the price of airline tickets than for comparing the price of health-care services. When consumers—employees—have the appropriate information, they can make good consumer decisions.

Employers have tried to provide employees with health-care information and have turned to their insurance carriers, disease management programs, or pharmacy benefits managers to assume some of the responsibility for educating employees. But the difficulty with this approach is that too many vendors are involved in the process. For example, an employee would have to contact the insurance carrier to get information to make one decision, the pharmacy benefits manager to get prescription drugs, and the disease management company for information about how to best manage a specific condition. Needless to say, it is time-consuming and frustrating for employees to have to orchestrate all of these different components. Many don't even know the right questions to ask.

Our economy has empowered the consumer with information on nearly every kind of product and its features, benefits, and price. As consumers, we have options for uncovering how products and services are rated so we can make informed decisions about what we want to buy and how much we're willing to pay—except when it comes to purchasing health care.

Employer Attempts at Transparency

The level of transparency in health care has not evolved because a gap remains in an employer's ability to convey the same level of information to its employees as in other aspects of the marketplace. One reason for this is that too much information is siloed; that information is separate and is not integrated into a comprehensive framework. Another reason is that employers haven't been able to get the right tools in place. Employers have invested in external medical and wellness portals or internal portals to help communicate health information, but the use of these portals by employees has been disappointing.

Employers have also implemented health risk assessments or other tools to capture information about employees' lifestyles as a way to understand how to help them adopt healthier behaviors. However, providing the right incentives to motivate employees to adopt these tools has been limited to less than 20–30 percent of a workforce.

Employers have been challenged by finding the right monetary incentives necessary to engage employees in specific health promotion programs. It's not enough for them to fill out a health risk assessment or a survey one time; a better method is needed for helping them manage their care in a meaningful way. Employees need to a way to evaluate whether the programs are working.

Programs Differ by Industry

Up until now, employers haven't had the information they need to help them understand what kinds of health promotion programs they should be investing in and at what levels to provide the most benefit.

Health program management varies by the age demographic of the employee population and by turnover rate. Not every company will implement the same program, and not every company will address it in the same way. Turnover rates are different by industry, and for some businesses, such as fast-food restaurants or retail stores, turnover can be as high as 70–80 percent per year.

For example, a manufacturing company, where employees remain longer or where there is a large number of retirees, needs to explore a different kind of health plan design, disease management program, or wellness program than would a retail company, where a majority of employees move on to other jobs.

Should companies with a high turnover rate invest in employees who will leave and join another employer?

Employers need to consider the impact of their industry's turnover rate on their health benefits. They need to evaluate the risk of their employee population in relation to the turnover rates for their industry to help them determine the investment they should make on the basis of that health risk and what kind of health programs they should be offering.

Retailers address health benefits differently because employees don't stay as long as they do in some other industries. However, these companies ought to be investing in their employees' health with something such as a disease management program because, on the basis of the concept of regression to the mean, or the law of averages, those employees will be hired by another employer but in the same industry. So, over time, employers will be addressing the same problem with different employees.

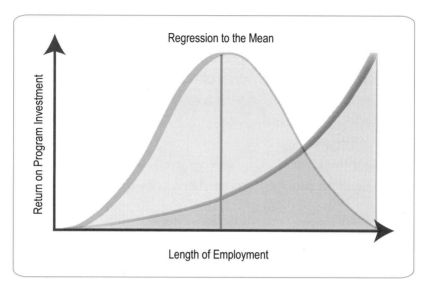

3.6   Turnover Rates v. Regression

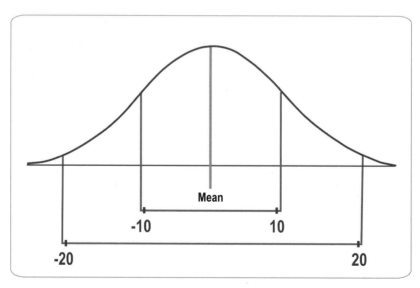

3.7   What Does "Regression to the Mean" Really Mean?

Many large retailers are reluctant to invest in disease management programs when these employees may not be with the company for the long term. Why invest a large amount of money in managing diabetes for this population when a year from now they'll be a competitor's employees?

The answer to that question is that making that investment is important. Employers tend to hire employees from similar demographics or the same distribution of individuals. This means that an employer's investment in health care will have an impact on the population, just not in the same time frame as a company with a lower turnover rate.

This occurs because of the phenomenon of regression to the mean, the statistical concept where data points, in this instance individuals, move toward the center of a distribution. Companies need to consider the demographic they're hiring and the risk pool associated with their industry and evaluate those distributions. Because of regression to the mean, investments in health promotion programs are justified.

Consider a simple example: A class of students takes a 100-item true/false test on a subject. Suppose that all students choose randomly on all questions. Then, each student's score would be a realization of one of a set of i.i.d. random variables with a mean of 50. Naturally, some students will score substantially above 50 and some substantially below 50 just by chance. If one takes only the top-scoring 10% of the students and gives them a second test on which they again guess on all items, the mean score would again be expected to be close to 50. Thus, the mean of these students would "regress" all the way back to the mean of all students who took the original test. No matter what a student scores on the original test, the best prediction of their score on second test is 50. If there were no luck or random guessing involved in the answers supplied by students to the test questions, then all students would score the same on the second test as they scored on the original test, and there would be no regression toward the mean. Similarly in evaluating populations for incidence of illness, one can expect such a distribution of individuals with a certain diagnosis that will happen over time by random sampling. As a result companies will ultimately benefit from investing in programs over a period of time-the time interval will vary based on the industry, turnover rates and demographics of the population.

Turnover Rate

Companies should time their investment in programs or strategies based on their turnover rates and demographics of the population. A retailer with higher turnover may initially invest more in wellness programs, whereas a defense contractor would invest in disease management. On the basis of the concept of regression to the mean, all companies will benefit from investing in all programs but should time their investments accordingly.

Companies weighing the economics of how to best invest in their employees' health care should base their decisions on the health risk, the financial risk, and the turnover rate for their industry segment.

Transparency Aids Union Negotiations for Health-Care Benefits

Executives in industries with unionized workers have an added challenge in balancing employee expectations. Negotiating benefits at contract time is difficult because of the limited transparency between the two sides regarding the actual cost of the benefits. We've already seen example of companies that had to deal with striking workers because of their reluctance to absorb higher health-care costs.

However, with transparency have come significant advances in union negotiations. As one example, a defense contractor was negotiating with one of its unions on the issue of health-care benefits. While at the negotiating table, the company was able to model the health benefit changes the union was requesting and share the implications of those changes. The contractor completed a real-time statistical analysis to demonstrate that what the union was requesting was more expensive than what the contractor was requesting. The two sides came to a quick resolution in removing this as an issue instead of completing tenuous negotiations.

Chapter 3—Key Issues

- Companies are caught in the middle when it comes to balancing shareholder and employee expectations. They're concerned about how far they can push the envelope for optimizing health-care cost versus health-care quality.

- Shareholders expect financial transparency in the future liability for health-care costs, how the liability will be paid, and its impact on corporate performance. The complexity of the health benefits supply chain makes transparency difficult.

- There is an increased need for greater sensitivity in measuring future liability because of its impact on earnings. Earnings per share is the ultimate measure of corporate performance.

- CFOs need to use the total health-care-cost equation to determine the company's health benefits liability. The total health-care-cost equation includes all of the direct spending on health care plus all of the indirect costs.

Chapter 3—Endnotes

1   J. Gabel et al., "Job-Based Health Insurance in 2001: Inflation Hits Double Digits, Managed Care Retreats," Health Affairs 20, no. 5 (Sept.–Oct. 2001): 180–186.

2   J. Gabel et al., "Job-Based Health Insurance in 2001: Inflation Hits Double Digits, Managed Care Retreats," Health Affairs 20, no. 5 (Sept.–Oct. 2001): 180–186.

3   B. Mehlman, "Understanding the First Digital Business Cycle," Technology Administration, Remarks delivered by Assistant Secretary for Technology Policy at Progress and Freedom Foundation Technology Policy Summit, Aug. 20, 2001, http://www.technology.gov/Speeches/p_Mehlman-010820.htm.

4   *McKinsey Quarterly Chart Focus Newsletter*, "Will Health Benefits Costs Eclipse Profits?" Sept. 2004, http://www.mckinseyquarterly.com/newsletters/chartfocus/2004_09.htm.

CHAPTER 4

THE HEALTH-CARE-BENEFITS SUPPLY CHAIN

"Medicine is a science of uncertainty and an art of probability."

—Sir William Osler

E very successful company understands that leveraging its supply chain capabilities results in a strategic advantage. In fact, companies continually fine-tune their supply chains to control costs, drive growth, and gain sustainable improvements in their operating performance. These companies focus resources and investments on managing the supply chain to get end-to-end visibility across constituents—from vendors to partners to consumers. The benefits of these efforts include informed decision making, improved customer service, and increased profits from revenue sources. In these companies, every major business process is viewed and managed as a supply chain—except health-care benefits.

With the average Fortune 500 company spending almost $500 million a year on health care and with this amount increasing at a rate of 10 percent each year, companies could benefit from applying their approach for optimizing the business supply chain to the health benefits supply chain. However, compared with other industries, the health-care industry is fragmented and disjointed at every level of the supply chain, from patient, to physicians, to facilities, to insurers, to payers. Little if any information exists across these levels to demonstrate quality or service value from a purchasing perspective.

Companies have had to make multimillion-dollar health benefits purchasing decisions based on limited data because information is not available to help them make decisions based on value. The data at their disposal usually include provider name recognition, geographic coverage, and price per unit expressed as cost per employee. Payments are generally tied to transactions, such as services delivered, and not to outcomes, quality, or performance.

The procurement and delivery of health and related benefits should be treated as any other business supply chain, with analysis of inputs and purchases, continuous management of processes, and measurement of outcomes.

Health care is a complex chain of suppliers and buyers, and each link has its own motivation. Many efforts have been made to improve the cost and quality of health care; however, the change has never started at the top of the supply chain, from where the dollars begin to flow. Why can't companies replicate the successful supply chain push strategies of retailers such as Wal-Mart and JC Penney when it comes to optimizing their health-care benefits?

How to Balance Health Benefits Supply and Demand

Unlike other products that are purchased on the basis of demand, health-care benefits are bought by companies in a multiyear, generalized supply because they don't have sufficient data to gain an understanding of who will consume which kinds of health-care services, when they'll consume them, or how much of the services they'll consume. In supply terms, this "overstock" is then consumed by employees and their dependents over the term of the contract. Sometimes there is too much stock, sometimes too little, and sometimes the wrong type. Relatively simple questions about the costs of health-care services delivered to employees can be difficult and expensive to answer, even though millions of dollars in expenses may hinge on the response to any one of those questions.

Companies can apply some of the lessons they've learned in effectively managing their business supply chain by achieving similar capabilities, such as the following:

- Analyzing appropriate data that reflect the entirety of corporate inputs and requirements for health and productivity within the workforce.

- Identifying performance issues and high-priority problems when they occur and, at times, before they occur.

- Measuring the performance of plans, providers, and programs in an ongoing and systematic fashion.

- Relaying information to vendors and employees about performance, quality, and value.

- Using this information to drive continuous quality improvement in program direction, contracting, and workforce management.

The health benefits supply chain is composed of many different internal and external entities, including the finance and benefits systems, plan administrators, insurance carriers, hospitals and other facilities, physicians and specialty providers, consultants, and plan enrollees and their beneficiaries.

Unlike most purchasing functions that have been centralized in many companies, health benefits has a number of internal constituent groups involved in procuring the benefits. One group may be working on the health and welfare segment. Another group may be looking at the health and productivity aspect, another group keeping track of workers' compensation and disability, and still another group tracking the financing or accounting component of the benefits.

A supply chain of such complex arrangement is characterized by a lack of information transparency because each of these groups is using different metrics that affect the amount of visibility in the supply chain. Because of this lack of transparency, companies have difficulty managing the supply of and demand for health care, which affects the total health-care-cost equation. A clear picture of all of the direct and indirect costs of health care is needed to accurately calculate the total health-care-cost equation.

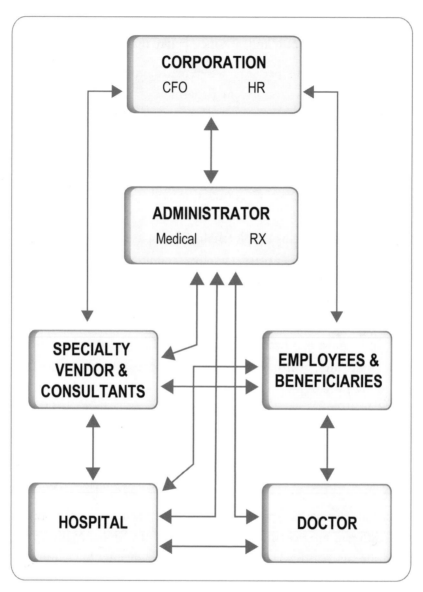

4.1   Health-Care Supply Chain

The external constituents present an equally complex arrangement of assorted vendors either administering the benefit or providing the programs. A company with 20,000 employees may have several medical insurance carriers, a pharmacy benefits manager, a disease management company, and vendors for disability and workers' compensation benefits. Each of these constituents is procuring and/or providing information or negotiating the benefits, but each is occurring in a silo.

In addition, an employer benefits consultant may be responsible for coordinating the benefits activities or for providing strategic guidance regarding the number and kinds of programs to implement. With so many constituents involved in the benefits process, it is easy to see why there is so little visibility into the separate functions and why companies have a difficult time gaining insights into the total health-care costs.

One way to get a clear picture of a company's total health-care cost is by effectively managing the two sides of health care: the supply side and the demand side. The supply side includes all of the benefits and programs provided to the purchaser, either the company or the employee; the demand side represents all of the purchasers' needs. An effective approach is to examine the challenges each constituent faces and look for opportunities to improve performance.

Supply-Side Improvements Focus on Business Performance

Unfortunately, in many companies, supply-side-focused health-care improvements are not prioritized, and benefits functions are unprepared to deal with the accelerating cost, complexity, and risks in managing benefits. The focus should be on business performance, with the goals being to increase transparency to effectively manage health-care costs, link analytics to strategy, reduce recurring variable health-care costs, and associate health-care costs directly with corporate balance sheet and profit and loss.

The top challenge for companies is the inability to link internal corporate and legacy systems with external vendor systems in order to generate performance information. For example, a company may have enrollment information in one system, lost time from work in another system, and payroll information in yet another system. While companies have spent millions of dollars investing in technology and infrastructure to support enterprise resource planning (ERP) applications to automate their finance or human resource function, they still have their health benefits information residing in many different systems.

In addition, multiple divisions of the company may be getting information from multiple vendors. For example, the human resources group responsible for managing health and welfare may be communicating directly with one group of vendors. Another group in the company may be working directly with the pharmacy benefits managers, and another group may be responsible for all workers' compensation or disability issues. The result is multiple groups in the company dealing directly with vendors and no crossover or sharing of that information among groups.

The finance aspect of managing benefits presents another challenge. In some companies, the budgeting and accounting functions remain in human resources, but in other companies, the responsibility for health benefits accounting is in another department. This means that the two separate groups are not able to get an integrated view of the information that could help them manage the supply side of health benefits.

Because the medical information isn't tied into the pharmacy information or the workers' compensation information, it's difficult for a company to understand its total health-care cost. The way the current system is designed, not enough information is available to make the best decisions around health-care-plan design, prescription drug benefits, or even how to evaluate vendor performance.

The metrics a company needs in order to make appropriate decisions are based on cost, utilization, and risk. The required systems also need to be in place to provide that information when needed, just as in a business supply chain.

Many retail companies use technology to optimize the flow of goods in their supply chain to create a dynamic process in how information is shared. For example, radio frequency identification (RFID) allows for remote identification and tracking of merchandise through radio waves. Retailers use RFID technology to transmit and receive data from one location to another; for example, when a customer purchases a blue shirt from a store in Chicago, the supplier in Hong Kong is alerted to ship a blue shirt immediately. RFID technology can reduce supply chain costs and manage inventory more efficiently. Hospitals are also using RFID to improve business outcomes and increase patient safety by tracking items through their supply chains, whether the item is an expensive piece of equipment, one surgical instrument, a prescription from the pharmacy, or even a patient.

Why, then, can't this technology be used to manage the health benefits supply chain? Enterprise technology could be used to consolidate information around enrollment, payroll data, lost time from work, and other financial metrics to create one integrated environment where all of the information could reside. This would create system efficiencies based on improved communication alone.

Once a company achieves an integrated view of the metrics across business areas and across vendors, it can depend less on vendors to provide that information. The entire benefits purchase-to-pay cycle can then be used to create more accurate forecasts and budgets, which would result in an improved return on investment. The metrics could

71

also be used to evaluate the effectiveness of health promotion and well-ness strategies and to measure vendor performance.

Demand-Side Improvements Focus on the End User

Even though the company pays the majority of the costs for health care, employees and their dependents are the end users who gener-ate the costs for health-care services. Reducing employee health-care-usage levels is an important strategy for managing demand and reducing health-care costs. However, demand-side savings are compli-cated by the fact employees make many nonoptimal health decisions that can have negative implications on their health and can result in increased health-care costs to the company.

Health promotion and wellness programs can reduce overall health-care costs by 10–12 percent by helping to reduce the incidence of health risk factors before they become serious medical conditions. The goal is to control demand of services by providing health-care education through disease management programs to the individuals consuming the most resources. But it is difficult for companies to determine the kinds of pro-grams to implement in order to reduce future medical costs.

Reengineered benefits packages, based on an understanding of value to employees and cost to the company, can cut health-care spending by at least 5 percent without impairing its perceived value by employees. But companies have to become more sophisticated in managing the supply chain in order to reengineer benefits to drive economic efficien-cies based on value.

However, an additional consideration is that companies need to assure that they aren't compromising the quality of their benefits while reducing costs. Consumer-driven approaches, such as plans with high deductibles, show the potential to reduce costs by 15 percent with strategies such as rewarding employee price and value comparisons,

72

providing financial incentives to choose cost-effective or preferred care, and educating employees so they can make the most beneficial decisions. But without the right data and the right tools to generate the right information and deliver it to the right person, efforts at managing cost and quality can be compromised.

Health Care as a Commodity

Increased transparency in the marketplace has made us all better consumers with the ability to drive down cost and improve quality. We can make decisions and choose goods and services based on the metrics we consider important, whether they are based on price, quality, or convenience. We can decide whether to purchase an expensive name-brand product or a cheaper imitation; a new or a used book; a direct flight or a long layover.

Becoming better-educated consumers has fostered robust competition in the marketplace. This is one reason why the cost of laser eye surgery has decreased since the late 1990s. LASIK (laser in-situ keratomileusis) surgery is a refractive eye procedure used to correct nearsightedness, far-sightedness, and astigmatism. Because LASIK is considered a cosmetic procedure, it isn't usually covered by health-care insurance. As a result, consumers use price-driven advertising to help them compare the cost and quality of the procedure. They can also search the Internet to locate qualified providers, study the newest laser technology, find pricing information, and learn about financing options.

Companies with improved visibility throughout the supply chain can also become better-educated consumers by gaining the capability to compare cost and quality of insurance carriers, hospitals, or pharmacy benefits managers. If companies are serious about reducing the cost of health care and improving the quality, they'll base their purchasing decisions on the three important metrics of cost, utilization, and risk.

73

- Cost is the price for the services delivered.

- Utilization is the volume of those services.

- Risk is the profile of the individual consuming the services.

When these three metrics are added together, the result is the total health-care expense of an individual with an illness:

Cost + Utilization + Risk = Expense

Companies that base their benefits decisions on cost, utilization, and risk metrics are in the best possible position to optimize their health-care costs. Instead of having the insurance carrier/supplier drive the health benefits program, companies can use information technology to gain insight for making better management decisions. By using the cost, utilization, and risk metrics, companies can identify employees who are at a high risk for consuming expensive health-care services and can then create personalized health management programs. The result is a healthier employee and a healthier bottom line.

In addition, companies that use these metrics can migrate their benefits purchasing function from human resources to the procurement department. At this point, the deployment of information technology becomes critical.

How Money Flows through the Supply Chain

To understand how money flows through the supply chain, let's look at the dynamics of four important elements: insurance carriers, providers, hospitals, and pharmaceutical companies.

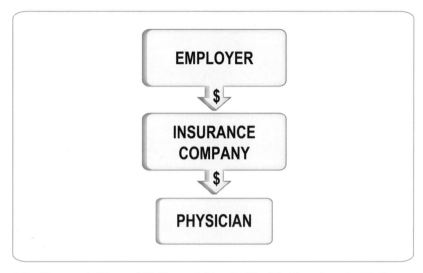

4.2   Economic Flow of Dollars within the Health-Care Supply Chain

Insurance Carriers

Self-insured companies bear the risk of funding the health benefits, but the responsibility for administering the benefit plan rests with the insurance carrier. The carrier is responsible for putting the right components in place to make the plan effective, including setting up the network of providers and the facilities necessary for providing effective health-care services.

One of the key challenges related to insurance is controlling the float, or the difference between the funds the company has in its account reserved for health coverage and the funds paid out of the account. Both company and carrier assume the risk that those enrolled in the plan won't consume the budgeted amount of services and that the float is leveraged as much as possible to maximize what is earned on the money versus what is paid out. This essentially places the company and its insurance carrier on opposite ends of the supply chain regarding the flow of dollars and how that float is managed.

Over the years, carriers have become more sophisticated in understanding how to charge companies to increase the float. They've learned how to manage the payments made to providers to optimize the float and ultimately the performance back to their shareholders. The challenges they've experienced have been the rising cost of delivering care, the increasing cost of technology, and competition being driven by other carriers. This has forced carriers to try to bring their charges down on the basis of what companies are demanding. At the same time, they've had to squeeze costs out of the system from the providers in what they're willing to reimburse in order to be able to absorb the competitive challenges that are being driven by purchasers. The carriers have become more knowledgeable about understanding the risk of the insured population to identify the appropriate provider networks and their efficiencies in order to optimize their margins.

Providers

While costs have been optimized in other parts of the supply chain, physicians have been squeezed from all sides. Reimbursement to physicians, especially primary-care practitioners, has declined over the years in an effort to control health-care costs. A physician can't do much to optimize charges, especially when the government continues to debate the amounts set for Medicare reimbursement. Physicians are now seeing more patients and spending more time with them, but they are experiencing a diminution in income.

A promising and more cost-effective model for reimbursing physicians is called the patient-centered medical home. Instead of being paid on the basis of the quantity of the services they provide, physicians are paid on the basis of the value of their provided services. The medical home model is one in which physicians are rewarded for managing their patients' chronic health conditions, including compensation for consultations and coordination of specialist care. Reimbursement is made on performance-based incentives and for reaching measurable patient health improvements. One of the keys to this approach is that physicians are active in providing preventive care and helping patients choose healthier lifestyle behaviors.

Hospitals

Another component in the health benefits supply chain is hospitals and other health-care facilities. They have been challenged in the amount of their reimbursement, the efficiencies of physicians providing care at their hospitals, the difficulties of giving care to patients without health insurance, and the rising cost of medical technology. All of these challenges have forced hospitals to become more focused on ways to drive their profit margins and how they can charge the insurance carrier.

Pharmaceutical Companies

Another important link in the health-care supply chain is the pharmaceutical industry, which is also facing a number of challenges. In addition to competition from a global market and government controls and regulation, pharmaceutical companies are under pressure to research and develop more products and bring them to market faster because of shortened drug exclusivity periods. Escalating research and development costs and declining market share, as a result of competition from generic drugs, are also causing pharmaceutical companies to restructure their supply chains. Even though direct-to-consumer advertising has made consumers more aware of new drug options, this doesn't necessarily translate into more profit for the companies promoting the prescription medications. Pharmaceutical companies have also recently faced litigation regarding several high-profile drug safety issues, including the anti-inflammatory drug called Vioxx.

Back to the Top of the Chain

At the top of the supply chain is the company paying for health care at the same time that it is attempting to lower the costs and improve the quality of the care. The company has been able to provide only some push back for what insurance carriers can provide, but companies have had little transparency in the efficiencies that go beyond the carrier. For example, how effective are the providers in the network that the carrier has put in place in terms of quality of care? How effective are the hospitals at providing care for the same risk of population? How are they measuring the efficiency within the supply chain? Companies have been limited in that visibility because the supply chain is fragmented and without a means for those data to flow between each link in the chain.

Ultimately, those who are paying for the care, the companies and the employees, should be connected to those who are providing the care, including the primary-care physicians and the facilities where the care is being delivered. But the route that employees take to reach their physicians is long and circuitous.

While efforts have been made to provide greater transparency to empower the consumer with more information and the trend has been toward adopting health information technology, most of those initiatives haven't been successful. Companies have tried to measure the performance of physicians, as in the pay-for-performance model, but that hasn't been effective because defining the parameters around quality was challenging and how that was being measured wasn't transparent. The Leapfrog Group surveys for inefficiencies in hospitals by compiling error rate data, but that's one siloed initiative that hasn't been integrated into the rest of the health-care supply chain.

Efforts have been made to look at individual components of the supply chain, but they have been disjointed. There is no consistent approach in the entire supply chain to allow companies to become better connected with all of the components, from insurance carrier to provider to facility. The key to linking the supply chain depends on managing the infrastructure and technology in order for this communication to occur.

It wasn't that long ago when core functions around procuring products and services were still being manually performed, even for large companies. But over time, nearly all of those processes became automated by using software programs such as Oracle and SAP. Technology allowed for more efficient processing and more transparency within the supply chains regarding the materials and goods they needed to procure.

However, within health care, extreme inefficiency has resulted from a lack of technology to link all of the components of the supply chain, and what technology has been implemented has been piecemeal. For example, electronic health records and technology for prescribing medications have been used, but the technology related to the supply chain is fragmented, and no common technology platform is in use. Another challenge to linking the supply chain is how information is disseminated. There are no consistent standards for communication between the company and the insurance carriers, the providers, the hospitals, the pharmacy benefits manager, or the pharmaceutical companies.

In order for the supply chain to be cohesive and efficient, technology must be consistently adopted across the supply chain. There also has to be a consistent standard for the transmission of data across the supply chain. This means that, for example, every constituent can receive the same claims data, that the data are coded in the same manner, and that all constituents can see the interpretation of those data in the same manner. At that point in time, we will be able to create a platform where the purchaser has greater visibility into the supplier and the two can come together to drive the best outcome for the consumer from a cost and quality perspective.

Additionally, all of the constituents need to have incentives to adopt the technology. It's not enough to be able to provide incentives for doctors to adopt electronic health records or for hospitals to adopt electronic prescribing; our standards for adopting technology need to go far deeper to achieve a universal standard. One approach would be for the government to provide incentives in the form of tax credits for health-care constituents to adopt technology standards. Although this may sound impossible, it can happen. Who would have thought, just a few short years ago, that we could have a single pipeline coming into our homes that would allow for every means of communication from telephone to television to Internet, through only one cable?

In the financial industry, the transmission of banking information follows consistent standards, but in health care, consistent standards don't exist—and that's where we create a tremendous amount of inefficiency for communicating information across the supply chain.

Because the supply chain, the information, and the systems are all fragmented, effective communication within the supply chain becomes nearly impossible. Laying that groundwork for communication becomes an important step in connecting the right metrics for how we're going to measure performance.

It's not enough to be able to empower hospitals and physicians to adopt electronic medical records. We need to address the inconsistencies that exist in other kinds of health data along the supply chain. We need a consistent platform, the appropriate health information technology, and the right incentives for all elements of the supply chain to optimize their processes, reduce costs, and gain the kind of visibility needed to drive real change.

Chapter 4—Key Messages

- An effective approach to improving the efficiency of the supply chain is optimizing the supply of and demand for health care.

- The goal for companies is to become dynamic purchasers of health care by balancing supply with demand. Companies should be seeking to drive vendor performance on the supply side and consumer choices on the demand side.

- Improved supply chain visibility is needed to allow companies to make meaningful changes in the cost and quality of health care.

- Companies that make benefits choices that reduce costs more than 15 percent may end up paying more for health care in the long term. Employees with chronic conditions may avoid appropriate care because of excessive out-of-pocket costs.

- Three important metrics can be used to better understand the cost and quality of health care: cost, utilization, and risk.

- With detailed metrics of what benefits the company wants to purchase, a central procurement function is possible for leveraging technology to control success parameters.

- Improving visibility between all elements of the supply chain allows data to be easily accessed and encourages collaboration between internal and external constituents.

- Consistent standards for how information is disseminated improve communication across the supply chain.

CHAPTER 5

IMPORTANT METRICS FOR MANAGING HEALTH-CARE COSTS

> "The very first requirement in a hospital is that it should do the sick no harm."
>
> —Florence Nightingale

E very link in the supply chain, whether company, insurance carrier, employee, physician, hospital, or disease management company, can benefit from understanding the three important metrics of cost, utilization, and risk. These metrics can be used to make decisions about which benefits programs to put into place and which to cut, which consumers to target for the most return on health-care investment, and how to measure vendor performance. The cost, utilization, and risk equation translates into better business decisions:

Cost + Utilization + Risk = Expense (CURE)

Cost (C) is the price of the product or service that's being delivered or consumed. This can include an office visit with a primary-care physician, a lab test, a diagnostic test, an inpatient hospitalization, or an ambulatory surgery. Health-care cost implies the metric of price for which a service is delivered. In most cases, that price has been established by various governing entities, such as the Centers for Medicare and Medicaid Services (CMS), which set the reimbursement rate for what the government will pay physicians or facilities for procedures or diagnoses. Self-insured companies commonly follow these same reimbursement rates.

As we've seen, the total cost of an individual with an illness includes the direct medical care to treat the illness and the indirect costs, such as sick time, short-term disability, and workers' compensation costs. These costs drive up the total cost of health care because any loss in productivity is a loss in revenue.

Utilization (U) is the volume of products or services that are being consumed. This includes any number of units, whether the number of visits to primary-care physicians or specialists, the number of outpatient or emergency room visits, or the number of prescriptions being filled or refilled.

Risk (R) is the statistical probability of expected health-care costs from the population consuming health-care services. In some of the country's largest employers, approximately 90 percent of their health-care costs are driven by 10 percent of the employee population. The primary conditions driving a preponderance of costs include diabetes, cardiovascular disease, asthma, low-back pain, and depression. The health-care costs related to these chronic conditions aren't driven by the primary condition alone but by a complication of that condition, or comorbidity, associated with that disease.

Risk is an important concept for estimating future costs in any industry. For example, if 100 drivers from across the country were surveyed about the cost of their car insurance, few drivers would cite identical rates. Each person's rate varies by demographic information such as age and geography, motor vehicle record, number of moving-traffic violations, number of car crashes, and other factors. Automobile insurance companies calculate insurance rates by analyzing these data to estimate the probability of the individual being involved in another accident, which would result in a loss to the insurance company.

Estimating policy rates by assessing the risk of certain events occurring is standard practice for setting rates in the insurance industry. For the past few decades, health-care-insurance carriers have used the metrics of cost, utilization, and risk in estimating expense (E) and for establishing the most cost-effective provider networks for their client companies.

Self-Insured Companies Assume All Financial Risk

In the self-insured health insurance model, the financial risk is assumed by the company and its employees, which is no different from the auto insurance company assuming the risk for its covered drivers. Shouldn't companies have the same level of detail about the risk of their insured populations as car insurance companies? The answer is a definite yes, but that's not how the current system is designed. Rates are set on an educated estimate based on actuarial tables and a high-level analysis of what the utilization was in the past and what it might be in the future. A premium is added, and that rate is spread across the entire company population without accounting for the metrics of cost, utilization, and risk.

If we took the same blanket approach to the 100 random drivers in the auto insurance example, every driver would pay an identical amount for car insurance. The rate would be based on a comparable group of drivers and what they would cost the company based on the average age and the average amount of money spent to cover accidents in the past. On the basis of this example, the drivers with clean driving records would pay the same amount for insurance as the drivers who have had multiple motor vehicle accidents. This example is not very different from how health insurance premiums are currently being calculated.

Cost, utilization, and risk are important metrics to consider, especially when a company of 20,000 employees is spending nearly $200 million in direct health-care costs. The indirect health-care costs may actually be double that amount, making the total cost of health care even more expensive, as it continues to grow at a 7–8-percent inflation rate.

When companies want to implement a cost-savings strategy regarding health benefits, how do they know where they can save money? Is it by implementing a specific plan design? By making changes to the plan design? Putting in place a disease management program? A wellness program? Changing prescription drug benefits?

Companies and their CFOs struggle to develop a solid business case that demonstrates that if the company spends x, it will save y.

That return on investment becomes difficult to calculate because the company doesn't have the requisite insight into cost, utilization, and risk. Depending on the cost-savings strategy that is being implemented, whether constructing a benefits plan design change or implementing a disease management program, every entity within the health-care industry is going to look at some permutation or combination of the three metrics to determine the impact on cost savings.

For any changes made in a benefit plan design to optimize that plan design, a number of questions need to be answered to determine whether the right groups of people will use the plan and benefit from it. "What is it costing the people in that plan?" "How many people are using that plan?" "What is the risk of the people in that plan?"

For health plans to be most effective, companies need to understand the metrics of the number of services that are being consumed, how often, and by whom; otherwise, chronically ill individuals may be placed in inappropriate plans.

CURE Provides Insight for Selecting Health Benefits

Companies have tried a number of approaches to reduce health-care costs, including promoting consumer-directed plans, reducing prescription drug benefits, and implementing disease management programs. Each of these attempts can result in reducing the direct costs of health care, but how can employers know whether these efforts reduce the total health-care cost? Companies may be surprised to learn that their efforts can actually increase their health-care costs and do little to improve the quality of care.

Because a preponderance of health-care costs are related to individuals with a primary chronic health condition complicated by another chronic condition, the cost, utilization, and risk metrics provide important decision-making tools for both employers and employees. Consider the example of an employee with diabetes who has developed, as a result of the diabetes, complicated retinopathy, a degenerative disease of the retina. This individual will consume a number of health-care resources, including frequent visits to an ophthalmologist and laser eye treatment.

Instead of using the metrics of cost, utilization, and risk for precise calculations, companies make health-care decisions by analyzing the total number of diabetics in a given population, deriving an estimate of services that may be used by the diabetic population in the future, and putting into effect a benefits plan based on that estimate.

If the employer places $2,500 in a consumer-directed health-care plan for this individual, or if the individual chooses to participate in such a plan, that amount will not cover the cost for appropriate care. This can result in more out-of-pocket costs for the employee and perhaps reduced productivity at work. If the employee neglects care because the cost of care is unaffordable, the resulting consequences could be severe and long lasting.

This underscores the need for companies to fully understand the cost and utilization of health-care services before implementing a benefits plan. They need to know the services available for providing the appropriate care for employees with a chronic illness, how often are they going to need care, and what the complicating factors may be.

Prescription Drug Benefit Plans

The CURE metrics can also provide valuable information for employers considering options for the company's prescription drug benefit plan, ranging from multitier formularies to mandatory generic substitution to help control drug spending. This limits the access to certain medications; otherwise, the costs of those medications are passed on to employees in the form of high co-payments or coinsurance rates. While this may cut the direct costs of prescriptions, it doesn't take into account the potential indirect costs.

For example, a number of patients have reported problems using the generic forms of some medications, such as antidepressants, blood pressure medications, and diabetes drugs, instead of the FDA-approved name-brand drugs. If an individual suffering from depression does not do well using the generic antidepressant, the company may have saved money on the direct cost of the medication but may pay the indirect cost of the employee being less productive at work, missing work, or requiring inpatient hospital care because the depression was not adequately controlled.

If companies take into account just the direct cost of their prescription drug benefit plans, they are looking at the cost in a silo and probably are not measuring the net benefit of switching from a name-brand drug to its generic counterpart. Without the CURE metrics, they are not able to get an accurate picture of the total health-care cost. This is also true if companies consider increasing the co-payments for medications without analyzing the indirect effects of that decision. Once again, companies can end up paying more for employees who can't afford their co-pays than they save by increasing the co-payments.

Disease Management Programs

Disease management programs can also benefit from using the metrics of cost, utilization, and risk for decision making. In the typical model for implementing a disease management program, companies ask their insurance carriers or disease management vendors to make recommendations for a program for their employees. Programs usually include a process for identifying the target population, setting practice guidelines, implementing a model for physician and support services, educating patients on how to manage their condition, and measuring outcomes in medical costs, pharmacy costs, length of hospital stays, emergency room visits, etc.

Companies usually pay to include every employee in a disease management program, but this results in excessive costs because the aim is too broad. It is based on an estimate of the number of individuals who may benefit from the program and an estimate of the return such a program could achieve. For a disease management program to be effective, it needs to target health conditions that can be controlled by an individual's actions.

For the employer, it's not enough to know the cost of the individual with a chronic condition, such as cardiovascular disease, or how many health-care services he or she is consuming or the risk of the other conditions that are driving that cost. Instead, what's more valuable is assessing the total cost of the individual who has had a heart attack and takes short-term disability. The most effective approach to disease management is getting the individual's hypertension under control and getting that individual working again and being productive.

Wellness Programs

Similarly, if companies are considering an investment in a wellness program, it is important to be able to assess the risk of their employee population prone to a health problem and consider what that investment ought to be. The amount of this investment differs by industry and by demographics, so it needs to be evaluated within the parameters of cost, utilization, and risk on the basis of turnover rates and the age demographic of the population to determine the total expense.

How to Measure Effectiveness

Companies have traditionally measured the impact of the health benefits they provide by using a variety of standard methods. The following explains another approach that both companies and employees can use to measure the effectiveness of the health plan design, providers, disease management programs, and prescription drug benefits.

HEALTH BENEFIT	MEASUREMENT CURRENT STATE	MEASUREMENT PREFERRED STATE
PLAN DESIGN	Measure the change in numbers of individuals enrolled in the plan; evaluate the amount of claims retroactively.	Evaluate changes in the efficiencies of the plan; measure comorbidity of illnesses; measure effectiveness of providers.
PROVIDER PERFORMANCE	Base P4P and provider profiling on clinical and financial measures.	Standardize methods for coding data; allow more transparency into performance data.
DISEASE MANAGEMENT	Use claims information to infer whether the program is effective.	Measure claims data; measure the impact of claims vs. the impact of the comorbidity of enrollees and compare with individuals not enrolled in the plan.
PRESCRIPTION DRUG BENEFIT	Measure the direct cost of medication based on claims.	Measure the direct cost; evaluate patient medication compliance rate and accumulated indirect costs.

5.1 An Evolution of Performance Metrics for Health Benefits

Health Benefits Plan Design

Currently, companies measure plan design by calculating the number of individuals enrolled in the plan or the number of changes in enrollment as employees migrate between plans. If a company changes a particular medical plan or has different options within a plan, then one method of measurement is counting the number of individuals that opt in or out. Another measure of plan design is a retrospective assessment of the number of claims dollars spent.

The preferred state would be to calculate the changes in enrollment but also to evaluate the changes in the efficiencies of the plan on the basis of the quality of care. Questions that help measure efficiencies include the following:

- How are groups of individuals migrating between plans on the basis of the risk of their disease?

- How are people with diabetes, hypertension, asthma, or cardiovascular disease choosing their health plans?

- Does an adverse selection or pattern affect these choices?

- Is the risk of an individual correlated with an illness (or illnesses) he or she has?

- How is the health plan selection affecting overall cost?

- How is the plan affecting overall quality?

The preferred approach for measuring a plan's effectiveness requires looking at the overall efficiency of the plan, as well as the comorbidity of illnesses. In addition, it requires measuring the effectiveness of the health-care providers and comparing plans accordingly.

Measuring Provider Performance

Pay for performance and provider profiling are currently receiving attention as health-care financing strategies, and some of the issues surrounding P4P initiatives were mentioned in Chapter 2. Before companies can start rewarding health-care providers for meeting quality performance measures, accessing meaningful provider performance data is a crucial first step. Companies have tried to be proactive in measuring the performance of their network of providers, but this has been difficult because of a lack of transparency in the data. First, provider data are difficult to gather for companies whose providers are spread out over a large geographic location. Second, patient data are inconsistently coded, which makes measuring the efficiency or performance of providers difficult. Even though companies have tried to be proactive with provider profiling, these efforts haven't been effective because of the inaccuracy of some of the data.

Companies that want to be able to negotiate directly with providers as a way to reduce health-care costs will need providers to standardize their data-coding methods and to allow more transparency into performance data.

Disease Management Programs

Currently, companies depend on disease management companies to propose comprehensive programs that will cover all of their employees. This proposal usually includes a guaranteed cost savings over a set period of time on the basis of the number of people who are engaged in the program. The only way to measure the success of these kinds of programs is to look at the claims information at some point in the future and to infer from those claims data whether a disease management program has been effective.

The preferred state includes measuring both the claims data for participants and the number of people enrolled versus the number of people who did not enroll in the plan. In this manner, companies can measure the impact of claims versus any impact of the comorbidity of those who have enrolled in the plans and compare that measure to those who have not enrolled in the plan. These groups would be stratified on the basis of a risk score that enables a company to measure whether it should be implementing wellness programs, disease management programs, or chronic care programs.

Prescription Drug Benefits

Currently, companies measure the effectiveness of a prescription drug benefit program by measuring the direct cost of medication based on the amount of dollars spent on claims. If changes to the program have been made, measures include how the direct costs have been affected by changing from a brand-name drug to a generic, from pharmacy pickup to mail order, or from a formulary to a nonformulary prescription drug plan.

The preferred state includes measuring the cost of the drugs based on the options that are provided but also looking at patient medication compliance rate and the indirect costs accumulated as a result of changes to the prescription drug plan. Indirect costs are measures of compliance and outcome for a chronically ill individual, such as inpatient visits or emergency room visits. Measures of both direct and indirect costs provide companies with the total cost of the prescription drug benefit as opposed to only a partial cost.

There are numerous economic evaluation methods for estimating costs versus benefits when determining which health-care programs to invest in. There is a difference between benefit effectiveness and utility when evaluating the performance of health-care programs. Below are some evaluation methods typically used along with an example of a cost-benefit analysis.

Cost-Benefit Analysis (CBA)

- Most or all benefits can be monetized (Assigned a dollar value)
- Intervention costs and benefits expressed in financial terms ($)
- Study results:
  - Net present value (NPV) = benefits minus costs, e.g., $1.0 million
  - benefit/cost ratio = return on investment (ROI), e.g., $3.00 to $1.00

Cost-Effectiveness Analysis (CEA)

- Benefits cannot be monetized
- Outcomes expressed in natural health units (e.g., per person achieving healthy weight, per smoker who quit smoking, per heart attacks avoided)
- Study results: (costs)/(unit of health gained), e.g., $1,000 per quitter

Cost-Utility Analysis (CUA)

- Benefits cannot be monetized
- Benefits expressed as a qualitative health metric (e.g., QALYs)
- Study results: (net costs)/(quality-adjusted life year saved), e.g., $50,000 for 1 QUALY

Source: Green, Fellows, Woolery, *The Economics of Health Promotion and Disease Prevention: Lessons from Tobacco Control*

Example of Cost-Benefit Analysis

- For every pound of weight loss across all employees, the intervention cost $75 per participant.
- For every added quality year of life, we spent $32,000.
- The company invested $200 per employee but saved $600, and so the ratio of benefits to cost is 3 to 1.

5.2   Economic Evaluation Methods

Short-Term and Long-Term Return on Investment

Defining cost, utilization, and risk means being able to lump together these three metrics and to identify how the metrics can be grouped to determine which cost-savings strategy is going to have the biggest impact on total health-care-cost savings.

Return on Investment Curve

Within the first 12–18 months, companies typically realize a return on investment for optimizing the direct health-care costs by making changes to their health benefits plan design, their prescription drug benefit plan, and their disease management program. This is the low-hanging fruit of ROI because these gains are easily attainable, but sustainable ROI is much more difficult to achieve.

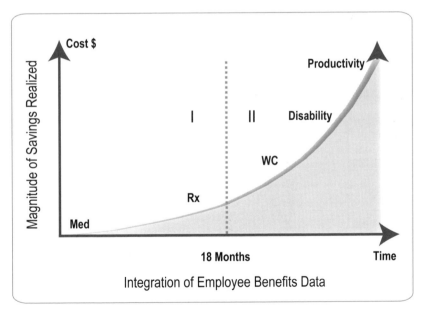

5.3 ROI Curve for Health-Care Programs

After the first 18 months, companies can optimize the cost and quality of their health care by assessing indirect costs, such as workers' compensation and disability-related issues. These costs are often captured in other areas of the organization and are not attributed to the primary condition, so they are never counted in the total cost.

An example of a company's success at continued ROI for its health benefits program, based on the total cost of health care, is Caterpillar Inc., the equipment manufacturer based in Peoria, Illinois. Caterpillar instituted its Healthy Balance program in the 1990s to promote healthier lifestyles and to reduce its projected health-care costs—which were on track to exceed $1 billion per year by 2000.[1]

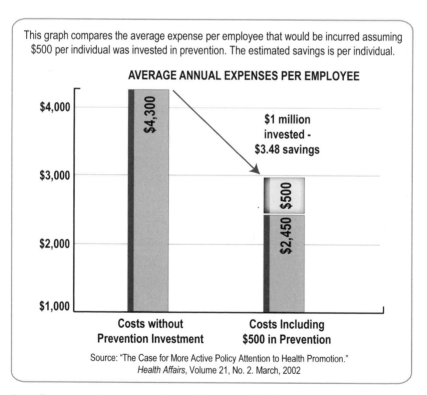

This graph compares the average expense per employee that would be incurred assuming $500 per individual was invested in prevention. The estimated savings is per individual.

AVERAGE ANNUAL EXPENSES PER EMPLOYEE

$1 million invested - $3.48 savings

Costs without Prevention Investment — $4,300

Costs Including $500 in Prevention — $2,450 + $500

Source: "The Case for More Active Policy Attention to Health Promotion." *Health Affairs*, Volume 21, No. 2. March, 2002

5.4   Return on Investment from Corporate Wellness

However, by the year 2000, the program was recognized for its effectiveness at reducing health-care costs and improving the health of program participants with a C. Everett Koop National Health Award. At that time, the program was anticipating a savings of more than $700 million by 2015.[2] The company achieved its results on the basis of the program's high participation rate, mitigation of risk factors, reduction in the number of physician visits and hospital days, decline in claims costs, cost savings by participants with heart disease, smoking cessation, lowering of body mass index, continuous quality improvement processes, and data accessibility.

The program's early success was attributed to periodic health assessments and interventions aimed at modifiable health risks, serial tracking, and segmentation into low- and high-risk cohorts, among other important elements. Interventions were especially cost effective in addressing the key areas of smoking, hypertension, exercise, stress, substance abuse, seat belt use, nutrition, obesity, and self-efficacy in health-care decisions.[3] "Participants who completed the high risk program reduced office visits and hospital days by 28 percent; a 23 percent decrease in direct costs validated by claims data."[4]

In 2007, the company instituted a Healthy Lifestyle Index in conjunction with the Healthy Balance initiative. By 2008, with 12 percent of the general population of employees meeting the index, Caterpillar had realized a 50-percent reduction in the number of disability days, according to the Center for Health Innovation. The company's value-based design takes into consideration the direct costs of medical care and the indirect costs of productivity losses resulting from the three major illnesses of heart disease, cancer, and diabetes.[5]

As companies move toward optimizing their health benefits programs, it is important to take a holistic approach for keeping each individual at work and productive. Many health-care costs, in the form of indirect costs, aren't considered health-care costs, but they should be. Most companies are unable to measure the impact of an employee who misses a day's work because her 5-year-old was rushed to the emergency room when his asthma was not well managed. There are no systems in place to factor in the total cost of the child's asthma, the emergency room visit, and his parents' lost day of productivity.

How to Define Success with CURE

How do companies know that their strategies to control health-care costs are effective? Instead of evaluating each strategy on the basis of the metrics of cost, utilization, and risk to determine total expense, the conventional approach has been to evaluate each program on the basis of its ability to control the expense of the health care and the quality of the care provided.

In the past, companies pushed to improve cost and quality by wringing efficiencies from within the system. In the early days of managed care, the health maintenance organizations (HMOs) were given the responsibility to control costs by having companies pay a fixed amount, and, in turn, the HMO controlled the care. To optimize cost, the HMOs limited physician reimbursement on the basis of rigid metrics without looking at the risk of the population or the volume of services being consumed. The result was that utilization of services reached a point where those with high risk weren't getting the right care and costs increased because diagnoses were being missed. What should have been an efficient system to cut costs by decreasing physician reimbursement turned into a system that increased costs because the population driving the preponderance of costs wasn't apportioned the appropriate care.

If there had been visibility in the CURE metrics, there would have been a better balance in the cost and quality of the care.

Transparency Drives Cost and Quality

Consider how transparency has affected the purchasing of most products in the marketplace today. Consumers who want to purchase airline tickets have transparency regarding ticket price, additional fees, time of departure, seating arrangements, and special services. Transparency means choice. The person making the purchase has visibility into the costs and options, resulting in competition from an open market. Consumers also have visibility into the quality of the service, such as record for on-time arrivals, the age of its fleet, online complaints from other passengers, and other measures of customer satisfaction. Now more than ever before, consumers have better-defined and more meaningful metrics.

Consumers can also benefit from increased transparency in health care if they are first provided with information regarding cost. Health-care consumers should have as much access to information about the cost of a coronary artery bypass graft as they do for the cost for LASIK eye surgery. The cost should be based on market rates, and expected outcomes should be explained. There should be information on hospital length of stay and lost time from work. Unfortunately, these metrics aren't readily available for consumers to access in order to compare services.

Educating consumers about the cost of health care is one thing; educating them about the right questions to ask about the quality is another. Consumers need to ask questions about health-care-quality indicators that measure outcomes such as patient safety and complication rates. This is especially true, considering how few of us even know the right questions to ask the automotive service technician when we take our cars in for repair.

There's a fine balance between providing the transparency and having the requisite knowledge to use it for making decisions. The educated consumer becomes the best customer by learning the cost of a service, how much is being used, and the risks. Ultimately, the best position would be the one where the individual who needs surgery is able to determine what that surgery will cost, the names of the top-rated surgeons, how much he or she might expect to pay if the surgery is complicated by a secondary condition, how many more additional services will be utilized, and the risk that will affect future purchasing decisions.

Among employers, especially those that offer consumer-directed health plans, the growing trend is to help educate their employees so they can translate metrics into meaningful information to make informed health-care-purchasing decisions. Until recently, the function of benefits has not been as focused on health care, finance, and technology at the core as it should be. Educating more company executives about the metrics and how to use them is as important as gaining visibility into the metrics in the first place.

Certain independent groups, such as the Leapfrog Group, focus on transparency for hospital error rates or infection rates. Other groups work to provide metrics for evaluating physicians or providers. But the information can be confusing when individuals try to apply it to their specific situation.

Companies have instituted health information Web portals that serve as gateways to Internet sites. However, it's not enough for consumers to have access to data; they need help translating data into useable information. One solution that companies can consider is tapping into the expertise of health-care coaches to help employees make better choices when it comes to purchasing health care.

The Government Can Benefit from Transparency, Too

For many years, the government has used estimates for making health-care-purchasing decisions based on life expectancy and actuarial tables for spending. Up until now, that's been a fair guide; however, estimates don't provide enough visibility for informed decision making. Using estimates instead of the CURE metrics is like using a compass instead of a global positioning system (GPS) to help navigate the complex system of health care. A compass can point us in the right direction, but the GPS will put us on the right purchasing path with pinpoint precision.

The government could have used more transparency in 2003 prior to enacting the Medicare Prescription, Improvement, and Modernization Act. This overhaul of Medicare was signed into law by President George W. Bush after a lengthy congressional debate and a slim victory based on a $534-billion price tag for the coming decade. In the spring of 2004, Richard S. Foster, Medicare's chief actuary, admitted that administration officials threatened to fire him unless he intentionally underestimated the cost of the program. In February 2005, the White House released budget figures that showed that the prescription drug benefit for this program would cost more than $1.2 trillion over the next 10 years.[6] This kind of creative math can be avoided with more visibility into the metrics used to calculate estimates of this nature. Companies can learn a valuable lesson from this government blunder by understanding that depending on actuarial assumptions is economically detrimental.

Do You Know Your CURE Score?

The important metrics of cost, utilization, and risk provide health-care consumers with data on which to base their health-care decisions. To truly be empowered, consumers need a means for analyzing those data, such as a CURE score. The CURE score is similar to a credit score, calculated on the basis of a person's credit history and accessed by lenders for approving a home mortgage, purchasing a car, or granting a student loan. The credit score is based on points for a number of different variables, including past credit history, amount of open credit, and other metrics to determine creditworthiness. Lenders use credit scores to determine the level of risk they undertake for approving the loan.

The CURE score is an index that reflects how much a person has spent on health care in the past, the likelihood of consuming

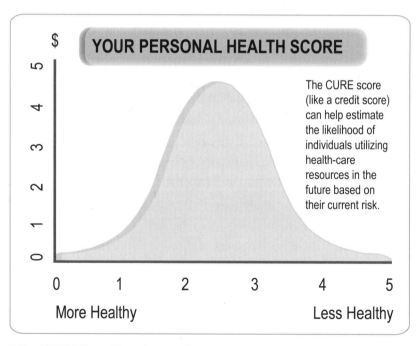

5.5   CURE Score Distribution Curve

health-care services in the future, and the parameters of the individual's risk for affecting costs in the future. This CURE score can serve as a metric for individuals to track their health-care costs and to evaluate health-care-purchasing decisions. The index can also be used by companies to track the quality and value of the health benefits they offer and to measure how well the risk of the condition is being managed or how the condition is progressing.

The CURE score is depicted as a normal distribution curve, with 0 representing a healthy individual and 5 an unhealthy individual. As an individual moves from risk score 0 to risk score 5, we can predict the cost of what a company might spend in the future. This takes into account the individual's utilization and risk to calculate the expense.

Currently, an individual with diabetes—or another chronic health condition—cannot predict his or her future health-care costs in order to make an informed decision when trying to choose from among an employer's health benefits options. However, the CURE score provides a method for measuring probable future costs.

For example, in the case of a diabetic, because the individual is on medication and has utilized services in the past such as outpatient appointments, an inpatient hospitalization, several emergency room visits, and trips to an ophthalmologist for treatment, the CURE score can help predict what this individual might spend on health care in the future on the basis of this history.

The cost (C) can be estimated on the basis of the direct costs of the past care, current medications, and other conditions the individual has, in addition to the diabetes, that are contributing to the chronic illness. The utilization (U) and the risk (R) are then combined to find the expense (E) in the future. The information can then be used to help determine the best health benefits plan based on the level of utilization of the system.

If you look at the normal distribution of a population, also referred to as the bell-shaped curve, it shows a preponderance of people in the middle zone who have a moderate risk of illness with multiple conditions. Companies can use the CURE score to implement the most appropriate programs and create the most effective incentives to keep their employees healthy and on the left side of the curve, as opposed to progressing along that curve toward the higher score on the right side.

This score can be of value when looking at certain populations or the impact of certain interventions and whether they are working on the basis of how the score is changing. It could also be used to help incentivize individuals to improve their score or prevent their score from getting worse. The value of the score is that it can be used by companies and employees alike to create a direct measure of health.

An additional measure could be factored in as the CURE plus score. This is the indirect measure of health based on productivity and lost time from work. Although this becomes more complex in calculating the cost related to utilization and risk, CURE+ is the total expense of the individual with a chronic health condition.

Chapter 5—Key Messages

- Companies need strategic information, delivered in a timely manner, to provide critical metrics used to implement programs and measure performance.

- Every link in the supply chain can benefit from understanding the metrics of cost, utilization, and risk as expense (CURE) to make better business decisions.

- The CURE metrics can be used to assure that the most appropriate health benefits strategy is implemented to reduce cost and improve quality.

- The CURE metrics can be used to measure the performance of health benefits plans, provider performance, prescription drug benefit plans, disease management programs, and wellness programs.

- The CURE score helps companies and employees alike create a direct measure of health.

Chapter 5—Endnotes

1   C. Everett Koop National Health Awards, "Overview for Caterpillar Healthy Balance 2000," http://healthproject.stanford.edu/Koop/Caterpillar/documentation.html.

2   C. Everett Koop National Health Awards, "Evaluation Summary for Caterpillar Healthy Balance 2000," http://healthproject.stanford.edu/Koop/Caterpillar/evaluation.html.

3   C. Everett Koop National Health Awards, "Overview for Caterpillar Healthy Balance 2000," http://healthproject.stanford.edu/Koop/Caterpillar/documentation.html.

4   Pennsylvania Department of Health, "Overview of Worksite Wellness and Its Value: Select Private Industry Worksite Wellness Programs," http://www.dsf.health.state.pa.us/health/lib/health/worksitewellness/WorksiteWellness-Overview.pdf.

5   Center for Health Value Innovation, "Achievements in Value-Based Design at Caterpillar Inc.," *Business Wire*, July 1, 2008, http://findarticles.com/p/articles/mi_m0EIN/is_2008_July_1/ai_n27877162.

6   C. Connolly and A. Allen, "Medicare Drug Benefit May Cost $1.2 Trillion: Estimate Dwarfs Bush's Original Price Tag," *The Washington Post*, Feb. 9, 2005, A01.

CHAPTER 6

MEASURING PERFORMANCE

> *"It is health that is real wealth*
> *and not pieces of gold and silver."*
>
> —Mohandas Gandhi

I n their efforts to reduce health-care costs and improve the quality
of health care, many companies have struggled with answering two
critical questions: how can performance be defined, and how can it be
measured? Companies understand that effective performance leads to
reduced costs, but performance measures for health care aren't as clear-
cut as they are for measuring performance in other industries that have
rigid parameters of success—or a lack of success.

Determining the performance of a car is easy because it can be
based on objective measures such as speed or horsepower. The business
performance of a company can be measured by the metrics of share
value or earnings per share. However, in health care, measuring performance is more difficult because of differences in quality standards
across the health-care industry. Each link in the health-care supply
chain has a different metric for what performance means.

For companies that aren't in the business of providing health care,
measuring performance becomes even more elusive. Some companies
have met the challenge of learning the business of health care; many
more have not, but they are able to do so. If companies are able to
evaluate their business performance on measures of how quickly suppliers can deliver merchandise or how many cars are manufactured per
day, they should be able to measure the performance of their health
benefits, especially if they want to affect change in their health-care
costs and improve the quality.

In the health-care industry, each provider has a different way of
measuring performance, whether through a physician, a hospital, or an
insurance carrier. For example, as a practicing ophthalmologist treating a patient with glaucoma, I was focused on checking the patient's
eye pressure, monitoring the visual function, and assessing whether the
optic nerve displayed any visible or subtle damage. There are objective
ways of measuring these conditions, either by observation or through

photographic evidence. At that time, I was focused only on objective measures of the condition to determine treatment success.

Now, I would also add that success is not only ensuring that the patient's condition is controlled by all of the measures to ensure that it isn't progressing but also assuring that the individual is able to be productive in his or her work and life as a measure of performance.

Physicians may be evaluated by hospitals on the basis of measures of efficiency in performance such as how quickly they can perform a certain procedure against a benchmark. For example, how long does it take a surgeon to perform a tonsillectomy or a coronary artery bypass graft? These are important performance measures because every extra minute consumed in the operating room adds to the anesthesia cost, the support staff cost, and the facility cost, which all add to the hospital's cost, the patient's costs, and, ultimately, the company's costs. Physician performance is also measured in the areas of clinical care, such as the rate of complications and the average length of hospital stay. Performance measures for hospitals include counting the number of preventable errors, injuries, and infections.

Performance Measures and Health Plan Changes

Historically, we've seen that one of the first strategies that companies use to control health-care costs is to make changes to the health plan design, such as switching from an HMO to a consumer-directed health plan. Many plan options place more of the responsibility on employees to make important decisions regarding their health care.

Most of the time, companies are able to measure the impact of the plan's performance by looking at the amount of the previous years' health claims dollars. If a company initiated a new plan, the only measure of whether that plan was effective in controlling costs is a review of the previous years' claims dollars to determine the changes in the amount of claims, the utilization rates, the overall cost incurred by the company, and the indirect measures of employee satisfaction.

However, more sophisticated companies have been able to look at plan design after the fact by looking at claims dollars and the risk of the population. Because risk has an impact on the kind of plan they implement, they also measure the plan's performance by the impact it has on the specific risks of the employee population. For example, individuals with chronic conditions, such as diabetes and hypertension, will have higher utilization and will need a plan that provides them with greater access to the right providers at a lower cost. These companies also measure performance by the population's comorbidities and the efficiencies of the plan to provide care.

Consider a company that has two plan options: plan A and plan B. With two plans in place, the company can analyze two groups of people with diabetes and high blood pressure. Comparisons can be made by asking questions such as the following:

- What is the difference in cost and utilization between these plans?

- Which plan has been more effective in providing care for each group of individuals at the same level of risk?

- How efficient have the physicians or providers been in each of those plans for providing care for that group of individuals?

Armed with these data, companies can approach their carriers with information on which plan is more cost effective and which plan offers a higher quality of care by the measures of visits to the physician, the hospital, or the emergency room. The bottom line for

PMPM COST, ENROLLMENT AS OF DECEMBER 2007 (PMPM - Per Member Per Month)

OPTION TYPE	# UNIQUE EMPLOYEES	# UNIQUE DEPENDENTS	ACTUAL TOTAL EMPLOYER PAID AMOUNT MEDICAL AND RX	ACTUAL TOTAL EMPLOYER PAID AMOUNT MEDICAL AND RX - PMPM	ACTUAL TOTAL EMPLOYEE PAID AMOUNT MEDICAL AND RX	ACTUAL TOTAL EMPLOYEE PAID AMOUNT MEDICAL AND RX - PMPM
HMO	24,831	44,180	$98,972,991	$120	$8,339,988	$10
Network Select	39,875	64,608	$190,447,398	$152	$30,622,492	$24
PPO	25,326	38,745	$79,755,443	$104	$31,475,228	$41
Total	**90,032**	**147,533**	**$369,175,832**	**$129**	**$70,477,708**	**$25**

PMPM COST, ENROLLMENT AS OF JANUARY 2008

OPTION TYPE	# UNIQUE EMPLOYEES	# UNIQUE DEPENDENTS	ACTUAL TOTAL EMPLOYER PAID AMOUNT MEDICAL AND RX	ACTUAL TOTAL EMPLOYER PAID AMOUNT MEDICAL AND RX - PMPM	ACTUAL TOTAL EMPLOYEE PAID AMOUNT MEDICAL AND RX	ACTUAL TOTAL EMPLOYEE PAID AMOUNT MEDICAL AND RX - PMPM
EPO	11,368	17,739	$63,025,620	$180	$7,529,022	$22
HMO	8,793	16,201	$27,981,232	$93	$2,470,589	$8
PPO	45,236	75,190	$142,188,731	$98	$37,571,265	$26
PPO Plus	22,905	35,987	$132,385,391	$187	$21,827,211	$31
PPO/HSA	1,730	2,416	$3,594,857	$72	$1,079,620	$22
Total	**90,032**	**147,533**	**$369,175,832**	**$129**	**$70,477,708**	**$25**

For this employer, this shows how one could evaluate the migration of individuals into certain options and the estimated cost to determine if the plan design was appropriate to both optimize cost and quality.

6.1   Enrollment Migration and PMPM Cost Analysis

114

companies is being able to understand which plan is going to provide the right care and the right network of physicians to drive the optimum cost.

Until now, companies haven't had that kind of visibility; they've had only limited details for measuring performance. They've learned in retrospect that some plans haven't met their expectations because certain demographics of individuals don't benefit from consumer-directed health plans.

However, the plan performance can be measured through means called migration analysis, which compares two databases and identifies the differences between them. This process analyzes the risk of individuals who are migrating between plans and measures plan performance accordingly. See Figure 6.1 on page 114.

A costly but important benefit offered in the majority of health plans is the prescription drug benefit, and companies have tried various options for managing its costs. These options have included adjusting the co-payments, modifying the deductibles, or changing the coinsurance from the employees' contributions.

Over time, companies have learned that reducing co-payments for prescription medications that treat chronic health conditions is an effective way to assure patient compliance. They understand the necessity of evaluating the impact of adjusting co-payments on the basis of the utilization of prescription medications, but they also make sure employees are educated, too. Simply making the changes isn't enough; pharmacy benefits managers also need to be involved in educating consumers on adverse reactions from medications or the advantages of using generic drugs.

Companies have also been focused on measuring performance as the total cost of the individual with an illness to make sure that the change in the prescription drug benefit is not causing adverse selection toward more utilization. This occurs because the condition isn't being managed as well. The structure of the benefits shouldn't restrict access or deter consumers from wanting to purchase the medication. For example, if the co-payment for a prescription to control asthma is changed such that it becomes a disincentive for the consumer to purchase the medication, the individual might accrue additional costs for a condition that is not controlled effectively.

A successful example of a company that emphasizes value as it relates to employee health benefits is Pitney Bowes Inc. The postal-products company revamped its health plan by choosing to provide more value to employees by lowering co-payments for all prescription medications used to treat chronic health conditions such as diabetes, asthma, and hypertension.[1] The theory behind this approach was paying more initially to control serious health conditions instead of paying more later in direct medical costs and the indirect costs of lost productivity.[2]

Employees also have more choices today when it comes to purchasing prescription medications. Pharmacies based in grocery stores and large retail companies offer prescriptions for a flat fee. With more retailers interested in the business of providing low-cost medications, such as Wal-Mart and Safeway offering $4 generic prescription drugs, we may see a dramatic shift in how medications are purchased. Companies that have traditionally contracted directly with the pharmacy benefits managers, who negotiate prices between the company and the pharmacy, may find that they can negotiate for themselves with increased transparency into the costs.

Predictive Modeling Is Economically Advantageous

What's been advantageous for companies when evaluating changes to their health plans is a process called predictive modeling, which creates a statistical model of future outcomes. Companies model changes, such as the prescription drug benefit, and evaluate the impact of each change in a "what if" analysis. "If we make this change to this benefit, what would be the end result?"

Modeling allows for certain parameters to be changed, such as repricing claims to determine what a new health plan would cost. In the past, companies would have had to hire a consultant to do the work, use actuarial tables for the estimate, and take several weeks to provide an answer. Companies can now analyze their numbers in real time, change the plan's parameters, and uncover the details they need in order to make a good business decision. This isn't very different from the process of applying for a home mortgage and determining what the monthly payment would be by using a mortgage calculator.

Disease Management Programs
Offer Promising Results

Disease management companies have been measuring their performance by evaluating how many individuals are enrolled in the program. One example of this would be having individuals with high blood pressure enrolled in the program and measuring their compliance in controlling their cholesterol or other risk factors for cardiovascular disease. They are measuring specific parameters, so they can issue reports on how the program is performing, but the real assessment of whether the program has been successful can't occur until after the claims data have been evaluated at the end of the year. Companies need to be able to look at the performance of their disease management programs on a much more frequent basis.

Prevention Efforts Improve Performance: McDonald's Corporation

McDonald's is the global leader in the quick-service food industry, with more than 31,000 restaurants in 118 countries, including more than 13,000 in the United States. More than 10,000 full-time employees are covered by the company's health benefits, including an additional 20,000 dependents.

Like many other companies, McDonald's has experienced escalating health-care costs, but the company remains committed to providing a high-quality program. The challenge has been keeping costs as low as possible for both the company and its employees. Bob Wittcoff, senior director for global benefits, is responsible for developing the strategic direction of employee benefits programs, and prevention efforts are at the top of his list. McDonald's understands that health-care costs represent more than just the cost of insurance alone.

McDonald's promotes a balanced and healthy lifestyle, and an important part of its prevention efforts is maintaining ongoing communication with employees. The company encourages annual physicals and regular checkups to track important numbers such as blood pressure and cholesterol levels. In this manner, employees have been able to identify health problems, such as high blood pressure, and receive prompt medical care before suffering a heart attack or stroke.

In 2001, the company began using information technology to make better management decisions regarding its health-care plan. Employees at high risk for future health-care issues were identified, and personalized health management programs were created. Because costs increase when those with health conditions are not getting appropriate treatment, a disease management program was implemented to identify either individuals who were at risk for becoming chronically ill or those who had been diagnosed with a chronic illness.

The company's early disease management efforts focused on such a large number of health problems that in 2008 McDonald's decided to narrow its focus. The disease management efforts are now concentrated on the most common and debilitating disease states, especially those where early intervention can have the most impact: diabetes, congestive heart failure, asthma, and several orthopedic conditions.

Short-Term Costs, Long-Term Benefits

The disease management program is voluntary, confidential, and managed by Blue Cross and Blue Shield of Illinois. Individuals are selected for the program by self-referral or by health data such as diagnosis of a condition, prescription drug usage, or claims history.

The program monitors claims data as a way to identify methods for helping employees better manage their conditions. For example, an individual with a diabetes diagnosis may be under the care of a general practitioner, but the claims data may not show visits to an endocrinologist, a best practice for

continues ▶

diabetic care. McDonald's is aware that using specialist care increases health-care costs in the short term, but the long-term results are more medically positive for the individual and financially positive for the company.

Measuring Performance

Program results are measured by reviewing the claims dollars of individuals who were not using medical best practices and comparing claims after they started following best practices.

Another performance metric measures the levels of wellness for individuals with the same diagnosis and compares the levels of those who participate in the program with those who do not. This allows the company to measure the program's impact to quantify results.

Results

McDonald's believes that results are based not only on financial performance but also on the impact the company has on people's lives, by helping them manage their own health care.

Many employees have written to thank McDonald's managers for offering the disease management program and have explained how their health problems were discovered early before becoming a more serious—and expensive—condition.

Vendor-Independent Reporting
Allows for Proactive Outreach

Companies would be able to measure the performance of their disease management vendors if they used the CURE metrics that are independent of the vendors' reporting. Companies can check the metrics of groups of people who have enrolled in each plan and compare these groups with groups that aren't enrolled in the program and evaluate how the costs and outcomes of the program were affected. They can conduct a real-time analysis and use the information to target their employees to help disease management programs become proactive in enrolling individuals into programs to manage their care.

Another consideration for disease management programs is instead of paying for every individual who has hypertension or high cholesterol as a risk for cardiovascular disease, the company should pay for a select group of individuals and manage their conditions better. By looking at the specific outcomes, companies can become more strategic in how to manage their high-risk populations as opposed to the entire population at a blanket cost.

A Blueprint for Developing a Business Case

For the HR executives who want to make changes to their health benefits plan design, initiate a wellness program, or add a disease management benefit, they need to build a business case based on ROI. Often the answer to a CFO's question concerning cost savings has been an estimate because the framework for performance measures has not been in place.

Company executives haven't been able to provide the level of visibility they need to make informed decisions about benefits changes because they haven't had vendor-independent reporting, and if they did have access to the information, it wasn't at the level of detail they needed, in real time. Measuring performance on any of these initiatives is tied to evaluating the cost related to changing the plan design, modifying the prescription drug benefit, adding a wellness program or a disease management program, and calculating the amount of dollars that were saved. In addition, the risks of the individuals need to be quantified using a methodology called resource utilization bands, a practice that's commonly used by insurance carriers to evaluate the impact of the risk.

Resource utilization bands (RUBs) are used to calculate the expected resource utilization for groups of people based on adjusted clinical groups (ACGs), which are categories of conditions coded by diagnoses. Lower RUBs mean that fewer health-care resources will be used; higher RUBs are associated with greater use of resources. This methodology for grouping clinical information can be used to group medical claims data, enabling companies to make decisions about health benefits strategies that need to be implemented.

RUBs typically range from 0 to 5, with 0 being the healthy group and 5 the chronically ill group with multiple conditions. This normal distribution shows that a sample of individuals from across the country would fall into the third risk band. RUBs give insight into the fact that most of a company's health-care costs are being driven by individuals with a condition and a comorbidity for other conditions. The cost for treating those conditions grows exponentially.

Currently, companies that want to invest in programs to manage the costs associated with chronically ill individuals have taken a shotgun approach by including wellness programs and disease management programs because they lacked clear data on where to apportion their resources; for example, they had no good data on whether

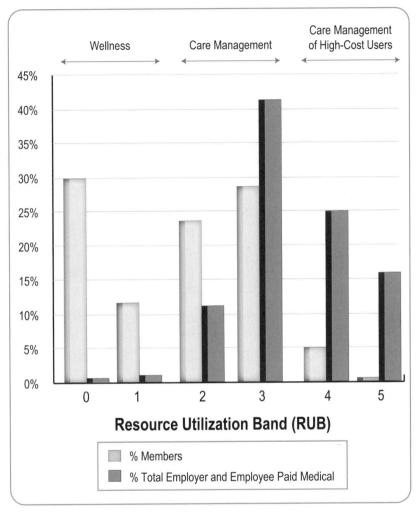

6.2   RUB Graph

investing in a weight loss program would be the best option for managing diabetes or whether a disease management program would be better for managing hypertension.

The distribution could vary somewhat on how the bell-shaped curve is stretched, based on whether that company is a retail company or a manufacturing company and the impact one could see on the ROI, whether on a short-term return or on a return spread out over a longer period of time. For companies that use the RUB methodology, it has enabled them to become more sophisticated in building a business case for the investment they want to make in any part of their health benefits program. This approach allows for understanding the cost and the expected savings based on risk distribution. CFOs can then confidently state, "If we apply X dollars to this specific area of this specific group, we expect these results in the cost and quality of the outcome."

Using this approach, companies can measure the success on an ongoing basis to know whether their programs are working. For some companies interested in changing the structure of their benefits plan, this approach may provide enough information for them to know their impending trend and how they can optimize top-line growth by investing in other businesses. For industries with a 1–2-percent margin, such as retail, even if they weren't changing their strategy, they could still get visibility into the future trends. Understanding the business case and its impact on overall productivity should help them decide where to invest and where they can recognize savings and impact profitability.

The Appendix found on page 246 includes the 11 steps for "Creating a World-Class Approach to Getting a Company's Health Care *Off the Dime*."

The CFO Scorecard

Chief financial officers could benefit by using a CFO Scorecard for improving benefits performance. The scorecard is a set of questions CFOs can ask to determine savings achieved from plan design, measurement of vendor performance, and evaluation of financial performance.

	PERFORMANCE ISSUE	MEASUREMENTS
PLAN	What savings should we expect from our new plan strategies?	Potential savings given demographics and usage patterns
	How have our plan strategies affected medical and pharmacy utilization patterns? What trends may erode these gains or reduce losses?	Change in prescription drug utilization Change in hospital use
VENDOR	Adjusting for all mitigating factors, who are our best performing vendors and how can we work more closely with them in other areas to take advantage of their performance?	Variations of cost, utilization, and quality across providers, plans, and vendors Use of preferred service locations
	How can we qualify our health risks?	Average risk factors in population and trend ROI on health promotion programs
FINANCIAL	How much are we overpaying in claims?	Invalid or inappropriate claims in invoices Financial discrepancies (e.g., charges, nonclaim activity) between claim and paid amounts

6.3   CFO Scorecard

It lists the kinds of metrics that should be tracked in an ideal situation for measuring the performance of each program. The CFO Scorecard can be used as a road map for how performance measures will impact corporate performance. Appendix B illustrates a sample CFO Control Tower of typical health care program performance metrics.

The scorecard includes the metrics for CFOs to understand the impact of specific benefits strategies and to track the ROI. For example, to evaluate plan design, companies need to look at the total cost of an individual with an illness, including what is being spent on the plan and what is being spent on productivity, such as lost time from work.

One performance issue is quantifying health risks by measuring the average risk factors in population and trend. General risks vary across industries, but sometimes risk results from specific activities that are unique to a particular geographic area. For example, many General Motors workers in Detroit, Michigan, enjoy the sport of deer hunting. Deer hunting in and of itself is not a health hazard, but out-of-shape workers with cardiovascular problems are at a higher risk for suffering a heart attack after bagging a deer and dragging it through the woods. In an effort to reduce hunting-related heart attacks and to keep a work-force healthy and on the job, the company has offered special conditioning classes for hunters in conjunction with its wellness program.[3]

A Corporate Index for CFOs

For the most part, CFOs aren't interested in the details of how many people with diabetes are using emergency room services or how many prescriptions have been refilled. However, they are interested in seeing a composite aggregate of important metrics and translating the data into a measure of overall risk for the population and productivity.

This would be an estimate of the impact to corporate productivity, shown as earnings per share.

A composite corporate index would allow CFOs to track costs on a continuing basis and help answer questions such as the following:

- How is the index progressing for individuals with chronic illnesses?

- How is the index progressing for the company as a whole?

- How is that number changing over time?

The answers to those questions can be a corporate indicator that confirms that the interventions are changing as a measure of how well the population's health conditions are being managed. Companies could use the corporate index as a benchmark or a comparison with other companies in their industry. The index could be used as a talk sheet of all of the relevant measures that CFOs need to determine what performance metrics actually mean.

The Corporate Health Index is a composite score to help companies better understand the health risk of the population and the likelihood of future utilization of services and its impact on financial risk for the organization. It can help executives understand the broad impact of the health risk of the population, the affect on productivity, and a quantitative metric that measures impact on corporate performance. The index is a composite risk score for a one-year time frame based on the members' ages, genders, claims data from medical and pharmacy usage, and any self-reported information from health risk assessments. The risk score is created using the Johns Hopkins Adjusted Clinical Groups methodology. A similar index can be created for employees and

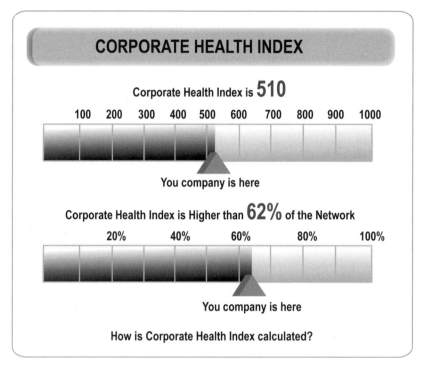

6.4   Corporate Index Sample

used like a credit score to help them track the impact of their health and lifestyle on future cost.

Using Performance Measures for Performance Guarantees

An important part of managing health-care costs is measuring the performance of vendors and holding them accountable for how responsive they are to service needs. Some vendor contracts include performance guarantees that measure vendor effectiveness and value. The goal of these guarantees is to improve vendor performance on the basis of measures that are indicative of the quality of care and service.

Most guarantees cover aspects of customer service, employee satisfaction, or quality of care for specific health conditions. Vendors are required to meet defined targets or provide refunds for targets missed.

However, companies have not measured vendor performance regarding the accuracy of the information vendors provide because companies rely on vendors to provide the information to them. Sometimes, errors are made in how claims are paid, as in duplicate payments or payments for individuals who weren't eligible at the time of service. This kind of information requires an ongoing and timely audit of the process to determine invalid claims.

In addition, companies have traditionally relied on insurance companies to demonstrate controls over information technology and processes in accordance with an SAS 70 audit.[4] Companies need more diligent oversight in order to ensure that no mistakes are being made, and, from a financial perspective, they also need performance measures to assure that vendors are meeting their guarantees.

Because more companies are taking initiative in requesting data from vendors and then aggregating the data themselves, there is a potential for additional performance guarantees that may include response time and consistency of the data as measures of performance.

Using Performance Measures to Ensure Satisfaction

Because health benefits are still considered a means of recruiting and retaining employees, measuring their satisfaction and tracking the outcomes are important steps, so that companies can assure that benefits are meeting this expectation. To this end, CFOs should be interested in evaluating how employees perceive their health benefits as well as how they select programs to better manage their health. In this regard, performance is optimizing not only cost but also programs and their impact on the outcome of patient satisfaction.

This includes measuring how much health care is being utilized and accurately predicting what the utilization will be in the future, as well as the impact on productivity, to know how health costs will affect the overall productivity of the organization.

One aspect of how to optimize the performance of health plans is related to the company's efforts to effectively market programs to employees. The challenge for companies is that they have strategic information about their programs, but gaps still remain in how well that information

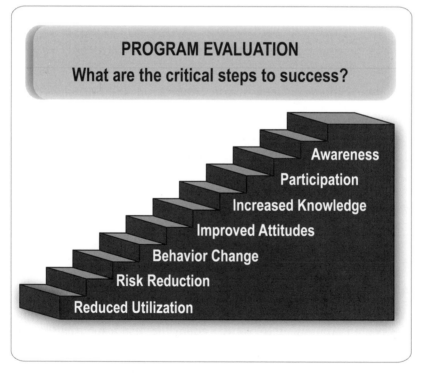

6.5   The Critical Steps to Building a Successful Health-Care Program

is communicated to employees. Can the performance of communication efforts be tracked? The enrollment of an individual in a smoking cessation program can be measured, but how can that program be tied to healthy outcomes? How has participating in the program reduced the likelihood of future utilization or costs? How can we evaluate that over time? How can we calculate the ROI for that program?

Companies haven't been measuring performance to determine the impact on outcomes of preventing illness, and that's when measuring the performance of programs becomes critical. The metrics for measuring employee participation show the impact of getting the right program to the right population to keep people engaged. If companies are providing incentives for employees to participate in programs, such as reduced premiums, companies need to measure the impact of those incentives.

Benchmark Information Based on High Performers

While companies have been focused on looking at specific metrics around incidence of conditions and number of encounters, it is more important for them to be looking at the impact of health-care cost on earnings per share and competitive advantage. Traditionally, companies have used benchmarks to compare their performance with that of other companies, either within their industry or within demographic norms, to determine how their cost trend compares. This can be used to assess the impact of the benefit burden on overall operational costs and its affect on competitiveness and whether they are above or below the norm in terms of what they are utilizing and what they are spending.

For example, members of the senior management team typically ask for benchmarks that may include a summary of the total dollars that have been spent for a group of individuals plus the average length of stay. Because companies have been struggling with their health-care costs

METRIC FOR BENCHMARK	CURRENT STATE	FUTURE STATE
COST	Total cost of illness	Cost per individual with illness by condition group
	Per member per month (PMPM) by facility, professional, ancillary	PMPM adjusted for illness burden
	Cost per encounter by inpatient (further by maternity, surgery, etc.)	Cost per encounter adjusted for illness burden
	Percent enrollment in health management programs	Percent enrollment in health management programs by risk group
	Percent change in benefits profit and loss expense	Percent change by risk group
	Total absence days	Health-related absence days per employee
UTILIZATION	Average length of stay (ALOS)	ALOS by risk groups
	Outpatient visits	Utilization of visits plus absence days
	ER visits	Utilization of visits plus absence days
	Compliance with prescription refills	Impact of direct and indirect costs of prescription plans
RISK	Total dollars by diagnosis	Total dollars by diagnosis and comorbidity

6.6   An Evolution of Performance Metrics as Benchmarks

with no dramatic improvement, we seldom find that they have been able to use benchmarks effectively in order to optimize a given strategy. To date, little has changed in the success of optimizing the cost and quality of health care by using benchmarks; instead, companies have gotten into the habit of using benchmarks as a defensive action.

If a company is only as good as its competitors in terms of their results, then another company's core results may not be the ideal benchmark. Companies should strive to compare themselves with high-performing companies that have been successful in reducing their health-care costs. High-performing companies are focused on managing health-care costs as a competitive business advantage; they manage their programs aggressively by looking for the causes that drive cost increases.[5] The characteristics of high-performing companies include identifying employees' health risks, implementing programs to tackle those health risks, and committing to helping employees manage their health care. In addition, these companies measure the effectiveness of their programs on a regular basis and create improvement plans when needed.[6]

Companies should be looking at the impact of health-care costs in totality, not just the direct costs but the indirect costs as well. They should be benchmarking themselves on the impact of health-care costs on earnings per share and using that as a measure of competitiveness. Currently, companies are looking at how their profits and margins are faring compared with those of their competitors, but they really should be measuring the impact of health benefits costs on earnings and profits as compared with that for their competitors. For example, if one company has had a 6-percent increase and the others had a 7-percent increase, that becomes less relevant, as opposed to looking at the percentage of impact it has had on earnings in the weighting of that interest.

Chapter 6—Key Messages

- Companies can and should measure the effectiveness of strategies designed to impact the overall health of individuals and the organization. Performance measures can be used to evaluate changes to the health plan, prescription drug benefits, or disease management program.

- Sometimes, paying more initially to control serious health conditions saves more money in the long run in terms of the direct medical costs as well as the indirect costs in lost productivity.

- Predictive modeling is an effective method for evaluating any change to the health benefits plan to assure that decisions are based on real-time information.

- The CFO Scorecard can help measure the impact of benefits strategies and track return on investment.

- A major component of optimizing health benefits plans is how companies communicate with their employees to help optimize the plan's performance.

Chapter 6—Endnotes

1   Center for Health Value Innovation, "CostRx: Investing in 'Human Assets,'" http://vbhealth.org/archive/archive/html.

2   Center for Health Value Innovation, "CostRx: Investing in 'Human Assets,'" http://vbhealth.org/archive/archive/html.

3   L. Hawkins, "As GM Battles Surging Costs, Workers' Health Becomes an Issue," *Wall Street Journal*, April 8, 2005, http://www.detnews.com/2005/autoinsider/0504/08/1auto-144408.htm.

4   Statement on Auditing Standards (SAS) no. 70 assures that a service organization has conducted an in-depth audit of their control activities and shows that the organization or vendors have adequate controls when the host or process data belonging to their customers.

5   Towers Perrin, "2008 Health Care Cost Survey," http://www.towersperrin.com/tp/getwebcachedoc?webc=HRS/USA/2008/200801/hccs_2008.pdf.

6   Towers Perrin, "2008 Health Care Cost Survey," http://www.towersperrin.com/tp/getwebcachedoc?webc=HRS/USA/2008/200801/hccs_2008.pdf.

CHAPTER 7

Issues of
Transparency

> *"America's health care system is neither healthy, caring nor a system."*
>
> —Walter Chronkite

The issue of transparency is at the heart of improving the cost and quality of health care. Transparency means that (1) elements of the health-care supply chain are visible to other elements, thus allowing for an open exchange of information; (2) companies don't have to depend on vendors to help them make important purchasing decisions; (3) employees are empowered to be proactive health-care consumers; and (4) all of the health-care-system players have access to the same kinds of information available to consumers of other kinds of goods and services.

The U.S. Department of Health and Human Services defines transparency as "a broad-scale initiative enabling consumers to compare the quality and price of health care services, so they can make informed choices among doctors and hospitals."[1] The federal government promotes value-driven health care for consumers because information will encourage all elements of the health-care system to provide lower-cost and better-quality health care. "Improvements will come as providers can see how their practice compares to others."[2]

The inequality of information that is evident throughout the health-care supply chain has created many of the obstacles we face in trying to optimize health-care services. The system is so complex, so unorganized, and so unmanageable that resources are wasted and patient safety is often compromised. In its 2001 call to action, the Institute of Medicine (IOM) published a report recommending an overhaul of the U.S. health-care system. The Committee on Quality of Health Care in America, which authored the report, recommended six targets, including the need for health care to be safe, effective, patient centered, timely, efficient, and equitable.[3] The committee recommended transparency to give access to information for making smart decisions when choosing between health plans, providers, or treatment options. Transparency ensures that information includes each option's performance as it relates to three key indicators: safety, evidence-based practice, and patient satisfaction.[4]

Insights into the Health-Care-Payment System

One part of the health-care system that could benefit from transparency is the health-care-payment system. The inefficiencies of this system account for at least 15 percent of every dollar spent on health care, amounting to a staggering $300 billion a year.[5] Much of the inefficiency can be blamed on the $250 billion that consumers pay to their health-care providers and facilities in addition to the $1.3 trillion in payments from insurance carriers.[6] The problem stems from the fact that transaction costs are so high and there is no efficient process for consumers to pay their providers directly. Despite the health-care industry's technological advances in the diagnostic tools it uses to detect health problems, its transaction processing system still remains in the dark ages. Who would dream that the majority of health-care payments are still performed manually?

The problem begins with the lack of visibility companies have for the dollars they are paying to insurance carriers. Further, insurance carriers don't have visibility into providers' costs. At the same time, physicians and hospitals don't have visibility into how payments are allocated and paid as reimbursement. The end result is that consumers are unaware of the cost and quality of the services provided to them.

One of the most important issues around transparency is creating visibility into the process of financing health benefits. It's enlightening to see how a claim is paid and how dollars flow through the system because the process showcases important implications for improvement by every constituent in the health-care supply chain. Currently, constituents, whether they are the ones providing services or the ones receiving services, are kept in the dark regarding how payments are made to the other links in the chain.

Gaining Financial Insight into the Problem

To get an idea of how transparency could improve efficiencies, looking at the problem from a financial perspective is important. The cumbersome method for processing health insurance claims causes problems throughout the entire process, starting when the company pays the insurance carrier to pay the provider for the care that's being provided to the consumer. From the time the dollar leaves the company and reaches the physician, there is little insight into how and when payments are made. The following describes the basic process for how a claim is paid.

A consumer schedules an appointment and sees a health-care provider. Service is rendered, and a claim is submitted from the physician to the insurance company.

The insurance company receives the claim, adjudicates it, processes it, and sends payment to the provider. The claim is simultaneously submitted to the company and the company's bank. Assuming that the company is self-insured, a request for payment is made. A hard copy of the invoice is received. The invoice is submitted to the company's billing department, a payment is released by the bank to the insurance company, and payments are posted to the company's ledger.

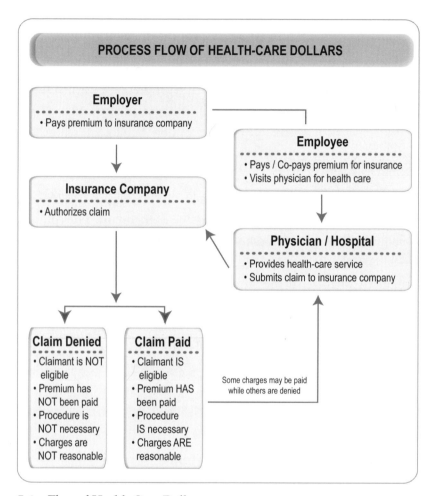

7.1   Flow of Health-Care Dollars

This example demonstrates what typically happens when a physician submits a claim. The insurance company has to first determine claimant eligibility and then determine whether the premium has been paid. If the claimant is ineligible or the premium hasn't been paid, the claim is denied. Another step in the process is assuring that the service or procedure was medically necessary and that the charges are reasonable. Some of the charges may be denied but others processed.

While the insurance carrier is examining the claim to verify whether the physician should be paid, the physician continues to provide care to patients, manage staff, and cover office overhead.

The process is further complicated by insurance carrier requests for additional information to complete the verification process. During this entire process, the money paid by the company to the insurance carrier sits in a bank account until that claim is adjudicated and paid.

At the same time, the insurance carrier is automatically debiting the company's prefunded insurance account. The money is held in a bank account that may be jointly owned by the company and the insurance carrier or the company and the third-party administrator.

The major difficulty with this system is that the company can't reconcile the invoices of what has been paid to the carrier. This would be like receiving a credit card statement with a $4,000 debit of the account without a summary of charges. Essentially, that is what is occurring between the company and the insurance carrier. Because of a lack of transparency, the health-care dollars that flow from the company to the physician must follow an intricate circuit of money management before the physician receives payment.

A transparent and efficient system would have a clear method for communicating the information on how those dollars flow through the system from company to physician.

Companies that self-fund their health benefits may be prepaying millions of dollars for health-care services that occur repeatedly without significant spending controls. Without proper controls and clear transactional data for these processes, expenditures are left unchecked, making financial audits a possibility. Companies need visibility into every health benefits transaction, from submitting claims to issuing checks to posting. Transparency like this can identify ineligible members, uncovered services, overcharges, incorrect payees, and diversions or duplications.

Health Information Technology Provides Visibility

One approach for providing transparency is for the constituents in the supply chain to adopt the use of health information technology to allow a free flow of information on the cost of services, the volume of services consumed, and the risk of the population consuming the services. Transparency is necessary across the supply chain in order to get greater leverage in optimizing the cost and quality of services and to gain accountability.

The current health-care delivery system does not provide a smooth flow of information that would allow constituents to improve their individual processes. Imagine if the grocery distribution system worked like the health-care system. The problems would start when the distributor sends a truck of products to a grocery store without knowing what kinds of goods are being purchased by shoppers. The truck driver would arrive at the store without knowing what's needed to stock the shelves. The grocery manager wouldn't know the cost of any items or what needed to be purchased from the distributor. Customers would walk into the store knowing the amount of money they could spend on groceries, but the items on the shelf would not be marked with prices.

This example is similar to what we're experiencing in the way health-care services are currently delivered. In health care, each link in the supply chain has a limited amount of information that it adds to the cost of care, and this imbalance creates chaos throughout the system.

The use of health information technology to exchange information can not only reduce the amount of chaos in the system but also improve care and reduce costs. The Center for Information Technology Leadership (CITL), a nonprofit research organization, reports that health-care-information exchange and interoperability efforts could save the country $77.8 billion annually, or about 5 percent of total annual health-care expenditures.[7] One specific example shows promise for avoiding complications from diabetes. The CITL issued a report on its research into the value of information technology–enabled diabetes management programs. The CITL found that using information technologies can improve compliance with standards of care; electronic provider–based diabetes registries can save more than $14 billion in diabetes-related costs over 10 years.[8]

Building a World-Class Approach to Health Benefits

Transparency in health care means that all links are equally empowered, creating the opportunity to build a world-class approach to health benefits using an eight-step methodology.

**BUILDING A WORLD-CLASS
APPROACH TO HEALTH BENEFITS**

9	Communicate Results throughout Enterprise
8	Leverage Technology as the Infrastructure
7	Improve Treasury Management
6	Measure Performance of Programs
5	Communicate Goals and Expectations to All
4	Improve Financial Transparency
3	Establish Targets and Metrics for Success
2	Open the Lines of Communication
1	Map the Supply Chain to Vendors

7.2   Building a World-Class Approach to Health Benefits

Step 1. Map the Supply Chain

The first step in building a world-class approach to health benefits requires an understanding of all of the constituents required to deliver health care. These include both internal and external constituents that have an impact on the benefits being provided to employees. Internal constituents can include the benefits function of human resources and the finance department. External constituents can include insurance carriers, pharmacy benefits managers, disease management programs, wellness centers, disability vendors, workers' compensation coordinators, enrollment vendors, hospitals, pharmacies, and care coordinators. Once the constituents are identified, a road map is created that includes all of the key systems where information is captured.

Step 2. Open the Lines of Communication

Once the road map is developed, systems need to be connected to ensure that the lines of communication are open to enable the information exchange that leads to transparency. The goal is to assure an automated, efficient process for exchanging information. The company's benefits, finance, and enterprise resource planning should be linked, as well as all third-party systems, to ensure rapid access to information and communication.

Step 3. Establish Targets and Metrics

It is important to identify and establish the most appropriate targets and metrics around quantifying the total cost impact and measuring performance. This can include assuring that the right health benefits plan or prescription drug benefit is in place. Once the metrics are in place, all of the constituents need to be aware of how the company is quantifying success. All constituents need to be open with one another about the expectations and incentives around the success measures.

Step 4. Improve Financial Transparency

A benefit of establishing performance metrics is that the finance department instantly gains transparency into what the company should expect to spend for benefits, the company's future financial risk, and the future trends and their downstream impact. Accurate estimates translate into improved forecasts and budgeting for specific programs or allocations for other investments.

Step 5. Communicate Goals and Expectations

Candid communication with the company's leadership team and its vendors is the key to transparency success. Clear communication sets the stage for what the company will accomplish.

Step 6. Measure Performance

The ability to measure performance and hold vendors accountable can occur only after assuring that each constituent knows the metrics and understands the company's expectations for meeting targets and the consequences for not meeting them. Metrics should be communicated using specific, measurable, and timely performance assessments; for example, vendor X is responsible for reducing emergency room visits for the diabetic population by 30 percent in the next 12 months. Transparency into the metrics is the only way to accurately measure performance.

Step 7. Improve Treasury Management

Holding vendors accountable to metrics means that the finance department can better manage financial risk and cost allocations on the basis of that performance. Improved transparency leads to improved management of the complex strategies of corporate finance.

Step 8. Demonstrate Results

The final step in building a world-class approach to health benefits is communicating to two important internal constituents: employees and shareholders. Employees need to see the results in improved quality of health benefits and reduced costs. Shareholders need to see the impact of improved health benefits on corporate productivity as earnings per share. For shareholders, the metrics that demonstrate performance include the following:

- Health benefits expense per employee per year

- Health benefits expense as a percentage of payroll

- Health benefits expense as a percentage of net income

- Workforce productivity

- Overfunding as a percentage of health benefits expense

- Overcharges as a percentage of health benefits expense

These eight steps toward building world-class health benefits enable companies to steadily improve the level of transparency. Each step in the process forms the foundation of the next step, allowing for an exchange of information between the elements of the health benefits supply chain.

As mentioned in Chapter 3, to enhance efficiency and communication within the supply chain, companies need the ability to link internal corporate and legacy systems with external systems to generate performance information. Companies also need an integrated view of all of the metrics impacting health benefits costs across business areas for vendor-independent reporting. In addition, visibility needs to be increased by linking the entire purchase-to-pay cycle for benefits to improve forecasting, budgeting, and financial reporting.

What Consumers Need to Know

It's unfortunate but true that the U.S. health-care system has created a group of consumers that expects a totality of services in exchange for their monthly premium and medical co-payments. And why not? Consumers expect the best treatment possible irrespective of what it costs because they don't feel that they should compromise when it comes to their health care. However, because of a lack of transparency, consumers have a disconnect between the cost of what they are paying for health care and the true cost of that care.

Consumers aren't able to make quality comparisons in health care, as they can when buying a new computer or mobile device, because expensive diagnostic tests don't come with price comparison charts. Consumers are not empowered to go to their physicians and ask about market rates for specific kinds of surgery or to log onto the Internet to compare the success rates of surgeons. Health-care consumers don't learn about price or quality with the current subsidized third-party system because of a lack of an incentive to demand this information—and the system isn't built to provide it, anyway. Only after the fact might consumers learn the price of a prescription while standing at the pharmacy or the cost of an office visit to a specialist when reviewing the bill. After-the-fact knowledge can't help consumers make informed decisions.

When consumers have no visibility into price, competition suffers by impeding the critical signals in a market for information about price, quality, and efficiency. Without visibility, consumers have few ways to find the information they need other than through word of mouth from family and friends or referrals to specialists from primary-care physicians who may not have information other than the fact that the specialist accepts the patient's insurance plan. These are hardly the best indicators for measuring performance.

Transparency Provides Insight: Pactiv Corporation

Pactiv Corporation is a packaging company best known for its Hefty brand products. Another large component is its food service and food packaging business, which provides packaging to restaurant chains and food distributors. Pactiv has about 8,000 employees in the United States, and, along with their approximately 10,000 covered dependents, they are covered by its health benefit plans. Lake Forest, Illinois, is home to the corporate headquarters.

In 2004, Mike Aldrich, director of total compensation and organizational development, wanted to make changes to the company's health benefits plan in an effort to contain costs and improve the quality of care. He used a predictive modeling process to estimate the effectiveness of health plan designs based on "what if" scenarios that anticipated outcomes based on each change.

Several plan designs were considered, including changes to the amount of deductibles and prescription co-pays. Changes to the prescription drug plan focused on reducing utilization of the most expensive prescription medications while still providing effective quality of care.

The process repriced the alternatives to give Pactiv visibility into the consequences of each change. In addition to evaluating pricing, the process showed how employees might react to the changes, such as the estimated number of those who might choose a specific plan.

Pactiv decided to offer a PPO with four different plan types and made these offerings available to employees throughout

continues ▶

the country. On the basis of information collected during the modeling process, the plans varied in the amount of deductibles and in how the prescription drug plan was calculated. Another PPO option met the qualifications of a plan that was eligible to have a health savings account.

Modeling also allowed Pactiv to segment its employee population by health status while maintaining the confidentiality of each employee's personal and health-related information. This aggregated data showed the company's current and future health-care costs. On the basis of health trend information, the company was able to make management decisions to implement a disease management plan and introduce new preventive programs.

Transparency Helps Reduce Health-Care Costs

One medical benefit option the company implemented was a coinsurance plan that gave employees transparency into the real cost of their prescription medications. The results were surprising. Those who switched to the high-deductible plan from the standard PPO were stunned to learn that their previous $25 or $40 co-payment for a prescription didn't approach the medication's discounted cost of $300. Because employees would have to pay this cost out-of-pocket, they began asking their physicians to prescribe equally effective—but less expensive—generic alternatives.

The prescription plan included a formulary that indicated a mapped progression from the generic prescription drug to the more expensive branded medication. Individuals had access to the formulary so that they could make informed choices about their prescription medication; they were also assisted by pharmacists who followed the formulary. Unless the patient had a medical reason for using the more expensive medication, the progression started with the generic.

Increased transparency also helped the company to set up its disease management program. Rather than relying on the estimated ROI provided by the disease management vendor, Pactiv could review confidential "blinded" data to compare utilization rates. An increase in utilization indicated that a participant in the disease management program was effectively managing his or her illness. Even though utilization increased and prescription drug spending increased, the company considered this a reasonable expense, especially when compared with the direct and indirect health-care costs for a poorly managed condition.

Managing Pactiv's Diabetic Population Is a Priority

Modeling also helped Pactiv recognize the need to implement a diabetes management program. Because diabetics have higher costs for medication and medical care and a higher risk for complications in the future, effective management of the disease can improve an individual's overall health and reduce health-care spending.

The company chose to participate in the Diabetes Ten City Challenge conducted by the American Pharmacists Association (APhA) Foundation with support from GlaxoSmithKline. The program has been proven to lower direct medical costs due to shortened hospital stays and to reduce indirect health-care costs with decreased absenteeism.

continues ▶

Companies that participate in the program provide incentives to encourage individuals to manage their diabetes with the assistance of trained pharmacist coaches and other healthcare providers. One incentive to boost compliance is that co-payments for maintenance medications are waived.

Pactiv has more than 40 participants in the diabetes management program in Illinois. Preliminary results show that more than 10 individuals have lost weight and reduced their medication requirements as a result.

Results Are Encouraging

Pactiv uses national benchmarks to measure the performance of its prescription drug plan. By reviewing the percentage of prescriptions that are filled with generic medications and comparing that number with past prescription use data, the company is seeing how increased use of generic medications has resulted in reduced pharmacy costs.

During 2006–2007 the company's trend for all medical spending was unchanged, based on a per-member/per-month basis. This is significant, considering an industry trend of 7–8-percent increases in employer-sponsored health-care costs.

Electronic Health Records Improve Efficiency

Efforts to develop an efficient system for exchanging information start with developing standards, such as electronic health records, and tapping into existing information technology. With the prevalence of sophisticated computer systems and databases, it is unbelievable that every time individuals visit their health-care providers, they must complete a detailed patient history using paper, pen, and a clipboard. Not only is this time-consuming, but also many times important information may be forgotten and omitted.

The technology exists for electronic medical records, but the industry is slow to adopt it. Instead, free services such as Google Health, Microsoft's HealthVault, and Revolution Health are providing consumers with the ability to create online personal health records and to store that digital information so it can be shared with their health-care providers. These initiatives draw on the popularity of the Internet to locate medical information to give consumers more control over their health-care spending.

All systems developed for electronic health records should be as easy to use as a bank's ATM system. Even though consumers use different banks, they are able to withdraw funds from practically any ATM in the world because banks are able to exchange information to allow these transactions to take place. The reason that the banking system works so efficiently is because it uses an interoperable system, and health-care information should follow suit. Like the banking system, the components of the health-care supply chain should have standards to allow the links in the chain to exchange information while operating independently—and competitively. Technology is the facilitator for information exchange.

In order for technology to be the driver for transparency, standards are needed for adopting technology and for transmitting information so that the method physicians use to code their patient information and the manner that insurance carriers process and transmit data are consistent throughout the industry, making that information easily accessible.

We need to develop the same kinds of standards that banks use to ensure consistency and accuracy. In health care, those standards would be used by all constituents in the health-care supply chain, from companies to insurance carriers, physicians, hospitals, and consumers.

Government Initiatives Give the Industry a Head Start

In 2006, President Bush issued an executive order concerning health-care transparency that was directed to federal agencies that administer or sponsor federal health insurance programs. Because the order was directed at agencies of the U.S. Department of Defense, Health and Human Services, Veterans Affairs, and the Office of Personnel Management, it affected about 93 million people. It also directed federal agencies to increase transparency in pricing and quality, encourage adopting health information technology standards, and provide options to promote quality and efficiency in health care.[9]

The executive order was built on four cornerstones for health-care improvement, including implementing interoperable health information technology, measuring and publishing quality and price information, and promoting quality and efficiency of care.[10]

A number of initiatives demonstrate how technology can be used to improve the delivery of Medicare and Medicaid services. These initiatives are designed to increase transparency into information that would give consumers the price of health-care services before a procedure instead of after the fact. In 2006, the Centers for Medicare and Medicaid Services (CMS) began posting information on what Medicare pays for 30 common elective procedures and other hospital admissions as a step toward transparency in health-care costs and quality.[11]

The procedures include heart operations, hip and knee replacements, kidney and urinary tract operations, and other medical procedures.

The CMS is also funding a project called the BQI project, or the Better Quality Information to Improve Care for Medicare Beneficiaries project. A number of collaboratives are participating as demonstration sites to test the pooling of private data with Medicare claims data, with the goal being to produce more accurate, comprehensive provider quality-of-service measures.[12] Pilot program sites are located in California, Indiana, Massachusetts, Arizona, and Wisconsin. In addition, a number of insurers are also beginning to offer their customers information on costs, clinical quality, and physician efficiency.

In a consumer-driven market, information competition is what drives change. When physicians have the opportunity to compete for business, whether cosmetic surgery or LASIK eye correction, the quality improves and prices drop. Transparency empowers consumers to make good health-care decisions.

Consumers can start by asking questions to get the detail they need to make their decisions, especially those with chronic health conditions. They should inquire about the medical costs of their care, including preventive health care, medications, special treatments or procedures, and potential hospitalizations because of complications from their disease. Cost is one indicator, but they shouldn't base their decisions on cost alone; they need to understand the risk of the population of individuals with the same diagnosis to help them set expectations.

Employees may have more to gain from transparency than their employers because the choices they make affect their bank balances and their health. Even the federal government acknowledges that when consumers can easily access information about health-care price and quality, they can make better decisions, and they should share in the savings.[13]

Transparency and SEC Reporting Requirements

As mentioned in Chapter 3, transparency is especially important to public companies when complying with financial reporting requirements. The SEC now requires public companies to be transparent when calculating and disclosing their total health-care liability, which includes the postretiree liability. Transparency, in this regard, assures that financial reports allow investors to make informed investment decisions and help creditors make important lending decisions.

The SEC doesn't look favorably on companies—or individuals—who violate reporting requirements. Civil fraud charges were filed in April 2008 against five former San Diego city officials for their alleged involvement in failing to disclose facts about the city's funding problems with its future pension and retiree health-care obligations.[14]

Chapter 7—Key Messages

- Transparency is the one issue at the heart of improving the cost and quality of health care.

- One of the most important issues around transparency is creating visibility into the process of financing health benefits. Companies could save millions of dollars by managing their health benefits procure-to-pay cycle.

- Physicians have few methods with which to measure their performance against their competition because they lack transparency into quality measures, too.

- Transparency can drive greater efficiencies by helping companies identify health-care-performance metrics and hold other links accountable for improving performance.

- Information technology tools can help companies develop forecasts in health-care budgets, track health-care expenditures, monitor the financial impact of health-care cost-reduction initiatives, and evaluate costs, returns, and paybacks for investment in workforce health and productivity.

- Employees who have access to information about the cost and quality of health care can be proactive when making important health-care decisions.

Chapter 7—Endnotes

1   U.S. Department of Health and Human Services, *Value-Driven Health Care*, http://www.hhs.gov/valuedriven/

2   U.S. Department of Health and Human Services, "Value-Driven Health Care," http://www.hhs.gov/valuedriven/

3   Committee on Quality of Health Care in America, Institute of Medicine, *Crossing the Quality Chasm: A New Health System for the 21st Century*, National Academies Press, 2001.

4   Committee on Quality of Health Care in America, Institute of Medicine, *Crossing the Quality Chasm: A New Health System for the 21st Century*, National Academies Press, 2001.

5   N. LeCuyer and S. Singhal, "Overhauling the US Health Care Payment System," *McKinsey Quarterly*, Web exclusive, June 2007, http://www.mckinseyquarterly.com.

6   N. LeCuyer and S. Singhal, "Overhauling the US Health Care Payment System," *McKinsey Quarterly*, Web exclusive, June 2007, http://www.mckinseyquarterly.com.

7   Center for Information Technology Leadership, "Our Findings," http://www.citl.org.

8   Center for Information Technology Leadership, "Our Findings," http://www.citl.org.

9   Executive Order 13410, "Promoting Quality and Efficient Health Care in Federal Government Administered or Sponsored Health Care Programs," White House News Release, August 22, 2006, http://whitehouse.gov/news/release/2006/08/20060822-2.html.

10   U.S. Department of Health and Human Services, "Value-Driven Health Care: Four Cornerstones," http://www.hhs.gov/valuedriven/fourcornerstones/index.html.

11   U.S. Department of Health and Human Services, "Medicare Posts Hospital Payment Information," news release, June 1, 2006, http://www.hhs.gov/news/press/2006pres/20060601a.html.

12   U.S. Department of Health and Human Services, "Value-Driven Health Care: Pilot Programs," http://www.hhs.gov/valuedriven/pilot/index/html.

13   U.S. Department of Health and Human Services, "Value-Driven Health Care," http://www.hhs.gov/valuedriven/.

14   S. Taub, "SEC Charges Five ex-Officials in San Diego Muni Fraud," CFO.com, April 8, 2008, http://www.cfo.com/article.cfm/11002450/c_2984379/?f=archives.

CHAPTER 8

CONTROLLING THE FLOAT

When Benjamin Franklin said, "Remember—time is money," he wasn't speaking about the American health-care system specifically, but that quote certainly does apply. Billions of dollars are added to the country's health-care bill every year because of inefficiencies in the billing system and long delays in the reimbursement system. One reason for this is that health-care providers process transactions long after care has been given. Another reason is that insurance carriers don't always settle claims in a timely manner.

During this lengthy process between service and reimbursement, each link in the supply chain has to find a way to manage its cash flow in order to remain in business. In fact, many businesses handle cash flow with the concept of managing the float. Float has different meanings for different parts of the cash flow system: it can be the amount of time that passes between a patient mailing a payment until the provider processes it, or it can be the time it takes the provider to process the reimbursement before it's deposited. Float is the time it takes for the deposit to clear the banking system before the funds can be used. It can also mean how much money is available for a company to invest or how much money employees have to pay out-of-pocket for their health care.

Every business has to deal with float in its own way, and some have discovered how to benefit from the delays generated by float. For example, banks will often hold out-of-state checks for as long as 18 days and collect interest on the money for that amount of time. Another industry that has found a way to benefit from float is the insurance industry.

Insurance carriers typically invest a company's premiums when they are collected, so interest is accruing during the entire time before a claim must be paid. This interest is so valuable that even when carriers experience losses due to a high number of claims, they can still realize a profit as a result of float. Because this is such a lucrative practice for insurance companies, they are always looking for opportunities to maximize that investment. The longer insurance carriers can hold onto the premiums, the more money they can make.

However, companies that self-insure their employee populations should be in control of the float. After all, the company's money is what's at stake, and the company is taking on the risk of insuring its employees. Companies can learn how to control the float to leverage it to increase investments instead of having the float benefit other sectors of the industry.

Two key approaches can aid a company in taking charge of the float:

1. Gain more detail in managing the health risk of its population by calculating risk on the basis of utilization instead of actuarial tables.

2. Disintermediate from insurance carriers and pay providers directly.

Health Risk = Financial Risk

Health Insurance 101

Before getting into the ways that companies can control the float, we should learn the basics of health insurance and some important terms. In health care, unlike other sectors of the economy, consumers—either companies or their employees—don't have the same visibility into what they're purchasing or what they're getting in return for their money. Much of the purchasing decisions are out of the consumers' hands, from selecting providers and services to making payments.

Companies that self-insure their health benefits take on the responsibility for footing the majority of the bill, but in essence, they have delegated the authority for purchasing the products to their insurance carriers. Insurance companies have been able to leverage this position to optimize the float.

Insurance carriers act as third-party administrators so companies are insulated from the real costs of health care. This approach to the marketplace creates an imbalance in the supply and demand for health-care services, and it has an impact on the economics of how health care is funded and on the payment mechanisms for how money flows through the supply chain. The third-party-payer system is the cornerstone for how self-insured companies pay for health-care services.

How Insurance Companies Make Money

The concept of insurance is the same across all industries, whether homeowners, automobile, or health insurance—it is a method of managing the risk of loss. Individuals and companies pay a premium to an insurance company to bear the burden of risk and accept any profits it makes from the transaction. As an example, consider the following hypothetical situation.

An individual with no health insurance has two outcomes in the coming year: stay healthy at a cost of $0 or become ill at a cost of $20,000. We assume that other individuals have the same probability of staying well or becoming ill and the same associated costs. The probability that each individual will stay healthy is 99 percent, and the probability of him or her becoming ill is 1 percent.

How would each person anticipate his or her expected health-care cost for the coming year? To do the math, multiply the cost of each outcome by its probability of occurrence for the total. If expected

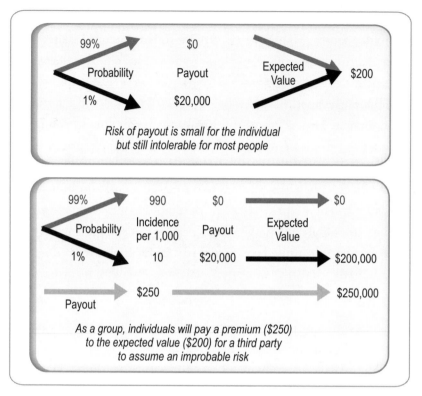

8.1   Illustration of How Companies Make Money

health-care cost is a probability of the first state (99 percent x 0 = 0) and 1 percent of $20,000 is $200, then 0 + $200 = $200.

Because this group of individuals earns more than $20,000 in wages a year, each person can afford the $200 expected health-care cost. However, no one individual's bill will be $200. For those who stay healthy, their bill will be $0. But for those who get sick, that bill will be $20,000.

If an insurance company offers an insurance policy for $250 to pay for all health-care costs for the year, most of the individuals in the example will buy the insurance because they are adverse to risk. They would be willing to pay the extra $50 premium over their expected benefit to eliminate the risk of having to pay $20,000 if they were to become ill. In effect, the consumer who is purchasing health insurance is passing the costs, with the associated risk of becoming ill, onto the insurer.

Will the insurance carrier be willing to offer the policy for $250? The answer is yes because carriers take advantage of the law of large numbers or volume. That is, while it is impossible to predict with any certainty the health-care cost for one individual for the year, it will cost the company either $0 or $20,000. If the insurance company sells one million policies, it can predict a total policy payout with some accuracy: 1,000,000 x $200 = $200,000,000.

Because the carrier will collect $250,000,000 in health insurance premiums, anticipated losses will be covered, with an additional $50,000,000 to pay for administrative costs and to provide a reserve in case claims are greater than predicted (and, of course, to make a profit).

Important Insurance Concepts

Several important terms and concepts are unique to the insurance industry, and having a basic understanding of the following is helpful:

- A fundamental concept of insurance is called the risk pool, where the risk is shared by a large group of individuals. The costs are spread over the group so that each individual realizes the average loss of the pool instead of the actual loss incurred.

- The two kinds of loss in the insurance business are random loss and definite loss. Random loss is the unforeseen or unexpected loss that occurs as a result of chance; definite or expected loss is what the insurance specifically covers, such as a car accident or a house fire.

- Risk transfer means that the risk is transferred from the insured to the insurer. Many companies choose to self-insure and assume the risk for providing health benefits to their employees instead of transferring risk to an insurance company.

- Indemnification means that the insured is reimbursed if a loss occurs. Within the context of health insurance, indemnification occurs when the insurer pays the insured in whole or in part with the expenses related to an insured illness or injury.

- Adverse selection refers to those individuals who purchase insurance because of a higher likelihood of having to use it. When a large number of these individuals buy health insurance, the insurer will most likely experience higher-than-expected claims, which trigger a premium increase. The healthier members of the group either forgo insurance or buy a less expensive insurance product on their own because they don't anticipate a high number of claims.

The Problems Related to Adverse Selection

Adverse selection exists because of asymmetric information, which results in individual buyers of insurance knowing more about their health status than the insurers—leaving companies with a majority of chronically ill members and no way to share the expenses with healthier members. Insurance companies attempt to control this adverse selection by the process of underwriting, where they refer to the selection and classification of candidates who they are trying to insure.

An insurance company can take two positions regarding adverse selection. The first position is that the insurer bases premiums on averages without considering the individual demographics or profiles of the individuals. In this manner, every person would pay the same health insurance premium, and the premium charge would be sufficient in aggregate to cover all of the expected outlays, plus earn a profit for the insurer. In this situation, their cross-up would span the population because the young, healthy, nonsmokers would pay the same premiums as older, less healthy smokers. After taking the administrative costs out of the insurance premium, the healthy individuals would be paying the premiums that exceed their expected health-care cost, while the unhealthy individuals would be paying premiums that are less than their expected cost.

The second position insurance companies take regarding adverse selection is charging premiums based on each person's expected health-care costs for the coming year. Individuals who are expected to have high health-care costs would be charged high premiums; those expected to have low health-care costs would be charged lower premiums. However, because future costs cannot be perfectly predicted, companies calculate the impact of the risk of the population and estimate the likelihood of future utilization.

Health insurers use two kinds of ratings to determine premiums and to protect themselves against adverse selection: community ratings and experience ratings. Community ratings are premium rates set for all members of a community without regard to age, sex, or health status. Premium rates reflect geographical differences and differences in demographic profiles, and the rates represent an average of high-utilization and low-utilization individuals. Experience ratings are based on the claims experience of the specific group of insured.

Companies with lower-risk employees will seek health insurance based on experience ratings. The least costly groups are skimmed from the insurance pool, and those that remain have higher-than-average costs. Because the health-care costs for those remaining are above average for the community, insurers serving that population have no choice but to apply experience ratings. Then, the higher premiums can be charged to the remaining group. The trend has been toward experience ratings and away from community-based ratings because that enables the insurer to help factor in those who have a higher risk and are more likely to drive claims in the future.

Another way that insurance companies protect themselves from adverse selection is by considering preexisting conditions. A preexisting condition is a physical or mental condition that the insured person has that existed prior to when the policy was issued. Insurance coverage typically includes a clause that states that preexisting conditions are not covered or are not covered for a certain length of time.

The Business of Self-Insurance

Many large companies decide to bear the financial risks associated with health care and self-insure. Companies that are self-insured assume the risk associated with the health-care costs and finance funds ahead of time based on an estimated risk of the population. The challenge has been that these companies don't understand all of the metrics to protect themselves against adverse selection in bearing their risk, and this has had an impact on their ability to control health-care costs. Insurance carriers are paid to administer the health insurance plan, but the company still bears the risk associated with cost and utilization.

The Irony of Self-Insurance

It's ironic that self-insured companies bear all of the risk for insuring their employee populations but they can't take advantage of the entire benefit of their insurance. These companies are paying a third party to control their float.

To gain control of the float, self-insured companies need to become more aggressive and learn how to manage the risk of adverse selection, just as insurance carriers do. If a company is going to be able to manage this effectively, it has to understand its risk. Until recently, self-insured companies haven't had the level of detail for managing risk and assessing how much money needs to be set aside at the beginning of the fiscal year. The amount is usually based on actuarial assessments, as well as on the rate set by insurance carriers. A better method is looking at utilization rates.

Because of the Employee Retirement Income Security Act of 1974 (ERISA), self-insured companies are exempt from state mandates governing health insurance, so they have flexibility in designing the health insurance plans for their employees. The company can set its own coverage criteria and the amounts of deductibles, coinsurance, and co-payments.

For a company trying to implement a plan for a younger employee group, such as in a high-tech or retail company, it may decide to set higher-deductible coinsurance and co-pays because the population may be paying lower individual costs. If it is in an industry with an older population, such as a manufacturing company or a defense contractor, the company may offer lower out-of-pocket costs but a higher premium.

Companies can also select their own third-party administrator as a means of getting some control over the efficiency of claims processing. However, the cost associated with implementing and administering the plan can be expensive, and the company is accepting more risk. This presents a significant disadvantage for small-business owners because a single catastrophic illness can have an impact on a small company; the risk cannot be absorbed against a much smaller group.

Self-insured companies need to have a more detailed analysis of their risk for two reasons: (1) the plan requires the company to free funds so that the carrier can make automatic debits and (2) the company receives certain tax benefits by prefunding into its account.

The challenge is that for some of these plans, once their money is in the fund, it is not available for other investments that may generate a higher interest. Also, if the estimated amount is either less than or more than required, the company may not be getting the full benefit of it.

For example, imagine if you were buying a house and the mortgage lender required you to prefund six months' worth of mortgage payments into an account so it could draw upon those funds automatically. If that money were deposited into an interest-bearing account instead of the fund, it might be generating higher interest. You would be losing out on the investment and the returns that money could be making. If the float was controlled for how the money was being used, you could make more money from the interest instead of prefunding an account over which you have no control.

This is similar to what companies are experiencing with prefunding. They are losing out on the interest they could be making on investments. A typical mortgage payment may be several thousand dollars, but in terms of a prefunded account for a company with 20,000 employees that spends $200 million on health insurance each year, the amount of interest on that would be significant.

Controlling the Float

A manufacturing company based in the Midwest has struggled for the past several years to better manage its health-care costs. From the CFO's perspective, the greatest challenge has been in managing cash flow and estimating and forecasting future expenses. The country's economic circumstances have led to continued volatility and unpredictability in costs—a CFO's nightmare. Finding ways to better manage the float has become a fundamental challenge.

In the past, "float" was defined as the time between when a check was written and when it cleared the bank. However, now the financial network is so automated and sophisticated that checks clear faster and this traditional float no longer exists. Float now has more to do with how the manufacturing company is managing the volatility of its money and understanding how much money is available on a daily basis. Float is the time when cash isn't sitting in anyone's pocket and therefore belongs to the last person who touched it.

For companies that have cash on hand, the main goal is putting that money to work, hence, the term "working capital." The manufacturing company CFO is attempting to keep a daily cash balance of less than $100,000,000 but doesn't want to keep this amount of cash on hand. His strategy is investing as much cash as possible every day. His finance department has used methods such as electronic lockboxes and time maps to match up when money is needed to pay out. When money is paying in that way, short-term borrowing is minimized.

continues ▶

This company's health-care costs have been escalating at a rate of 9 percent per year, and the unpredictability of these costs has caused the CFO significant concern. The CFO needs to understand the amount that the third-party administrator (TPA) will require for payment, as well as the timing of that payment so the opportunity for any float is better quantified.

The manufacturing company is funding a VEBA on a quarterly basis, based on the estimations of reserve provided by the company's consultants. However, for the past two quarters, the estimated amount has varied significantly from the actual amount, and the company had to borrow money in order to cover the shortfall. For a company spending in excess of $200,000,000 on health care per year on direct costs alone, even a 2-percent variance has substantial impact in terms of float.

In this situation, the TPAs and the carriers potentially benefit more by leveraging access to funds from the company prior to payment and holding onto the money as long as possible before making the provider payments. This is the same challenge many companies face in taking greater control of the float to maximize their return on capital.

Accurate Forecasting for Cash Flow

In addition to the loss of potential interest, millions of dollars can be prepaid for health-care services that occur repeatedly without spending controls. Without proper controls and clear transactional data for these processes, expenditures can be left unchecked. Problems can occur when claims processing errors trigger expenditures for invalid claims; when general ledger postings are based on inconsistent, incomplete, or unchecked vendor data; or when overcharges are hidden in batched invoices. Incomplete audit trails and reconciliation procedures can occur when companies depend on third-party information.

Because of the Statement of Financial Accounting Standards 106, accounting rules require companies to include the amount they have prefunded for their retiree benefits in the context of their balance sheets and to disclose how that amount is calculated. If the calculation was based on actuarial estimates instead of on utilization, the actual amount could vary significantly. This could have an impact on

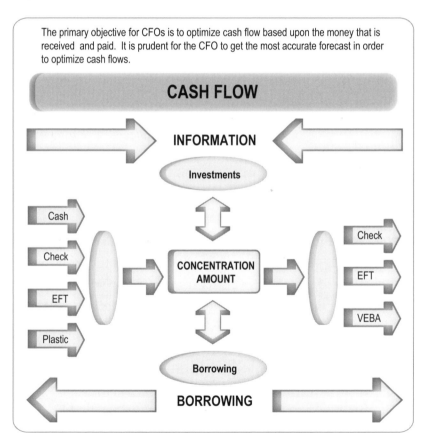

8.2 Accurate Forecasting for Cash Management

the financial picture of the company, especially where a 1-percent difference in that calculation has a large impact.

More accurate forecasting, based on actual utilization as opposed to actuarial estimates, helps companies understand the amount of money that can be placed into reserve or invested.

Companies Should Assert Their Roles as Buyers

Perhaps you may have realized that the business of employer-sponsored health care could be much more efficient if companies used their health-care dollars to pay health-care providers directly. Companies can gain control over the float by asserting their role as health-care buyers and working to improve the procure-to-pay cycle. The primary method for a company to assert its role as buyer is disintermediating the middleman.

As early as 1971, the John Deere Company, the manufacturer of farm and construction equipment, took the concept of self-insurance to another level when it decided to separate from its insurers. By the 1980s, John Deere Health Care Inc. had organized two health maintenance organizations under the name Heritage. The company continued to create a number of Heritage HMOs in several states, and at one time the Heritage National Health Plan had nearly 300,000 members from more than 300 other companies.[1] By 1993, the tractor manufacturer had opened a family care center near its headquarters in Moline, Illinois, to provide basic medical care to about 6,000 people, including its employees, retirees, and their dependents.

The company sought to provide higher-quality care at a lower cost by applying the same kind of management attention to its health benefits as it did to its core business. The company also set the goal to establish a new line of business by building and running medical practices.

It was so successful that it was able to sell its for-profit managed-care business to UnitedHealth Group in 2006 for $500 million in cash.[2]

Payment Timeliness Is an Issue

Physicians are the other link in the health benefits supply chain that would benefit from greater control of the float. Physicians lose out on the float because of the amount of time it takes between the date the physician sends a claim to the payer, when the payer first responds, and when payment is made. During this lag time, physicians are trying to manage their practices and cash flow. They are missing out on the float because they're waiting for reimbursement from the insurance company, and because the amount of reimbursement has dropped and the amount of lag time for getting reimbursed has increased, the value of physicians' dollars has diminished in the system.

According to the American Medical Association's (AMA) 2008 National Health Insurer Report Card, physicians are spending as much as 14 percent of their total collections to assure that their reimbursements are accurate.[3] Physicians experience problems due to health insurers and other third-party payers delaying, denying, and/or reducing payments, which can all add to the cost of health care. One example is the metric for payment timeliness, measured as the first remittance response time. This was measured as the median time period between the date the physician claim was received by the payer and the date the payer produced the first electronic remittance advice (ERA) or explanation of benefits (EOB). The response time ranged among health insurers from 4 to 14 median days.[4]

The traditional float cycle depicts the situation that exists for many companies, from when orders are placed to when payments are made.

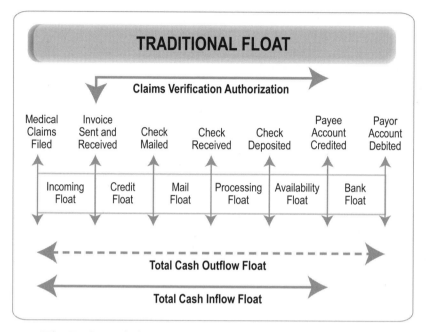

8.3   The Traditional Float Cycle for Health-Care Payments

Additional delays occur in this process because of the cumbersome verification, authorization, and validation of claims, enabling insurance carriers to further benefit from the float on money that is received from the employer and should be ultimately paid to the provider.

Self-insured companies that want to make an impact on their health-care costs and control the float need to disintermediate the insurance carrier and connect their health-care-insurance dollars directly to their health-care providers. The buyer should be directly connected with the individual or entities providing the services. Paying physicians and provider networks directly results in improved cost and care, as pay-for-performance initiatives demonstrate. Companies that become better at managing their risk are better able to leverage their float, and providers benefit by being paid faster, as long as they are meeting the objectives of providing quality care.

Research shows that delayed payment of physician claims can be due to provider, payer, patient, and technical errors, such as the provider setting up the account incorrectly, providers not following up on denials, and payers incorrectly processing invoices.[5]

Chapter 8—Key Messages

- Companies that self-insure should be in control of the float and should leverage it to increase investments.

- Two approaches for taking control of the float are gaining more detail in managing the risk of an employee population on the basis of utilization and disintermediating from insurance carriers and paying providers directly.

- The more detailed a self-insured company can get in understanding and managing the risk of its population, the better able it will be to allocate the necessary amount of funds to its prefunded account.

- When companies disintermediate from insurers and pay providers directly for their services, the results include improved health care and reduced costs.

- The government could also benefit from controlling the float in how it funds Medicare. The economics of the health-care burden would be better dispersed by understanding the cost, utilization, and risk of the metrics that impact float.

Chapter 8—Endnotes

1   B. Feder, "Deere Sees a Future in Health Care," *The New York Times*, July 1, 1994, D1.

2   "Deere & Company Closes Sale of Health Care Operations," Feb. 24, 2006, http://www.deere.com.

3   American Medical Association Practice Management Center, "Health Insurers' Report Cards Show Need for Improvement," 2008.

4   American Medical Association (AMA), "2008 National Health Insurer Report Card," http://www.ama-assn.org/go/healthatclaim.

5   C. Hollenbeak, J. M. Lundeen, and W. W. Souba, "Sources of Error in Delayed Payment of Physician Claims," Abstr Acad Health Serv Res Health Policy Meet 19 (2002): 15.

CHAPTER 9

Using Technology to Bridge HR and Finance

> *"It's the mind that makes the body rich."*
>
> —William Shakespeare

C ompanies have invested millions in enterprise resource planning technology to improve efficiencies for their internal operations, yet one key area still uses archaic systems to provide important information: health benefits. In agriculture, silos are used for bulk storage of one kind of grain, and that description isn't too far removed from companies that store their benefits and finance data in silos that can't be accessed from other systems.

Companies could be maximizing the value of their investments in enterprise technology by leveraging their corporate information technology systems to manage their health benefits programs. Enterprise resource planning environments contain disparate data residing in financial, accounting, and HR modules, as well as outside the company in vendor systems. Technology can integrate these data sources to provide increased visibility into cost, utilization, and risk metrics, providing performance analyses, trending and forecasts, financial calculations, and estimations across business units, vendors, and target populations. Suddenly, data become actionable information.

Leveraging technology creates transparency across the health benefits supply chain, and having an integrated view of expenditures has many advantages. But a number of obstacles create challenges in linking finance and benefits systems with third-party claims systems, such as a dearth of technology standards, a focus on using transactional data, information technology initiatives aimed at the wrong links in the health benefits supply chain, and human resources practitioners lacking insight into the complexities of health-care financing.

Fortunately, these obstacles provide opportunities for companies to make significant gains in their health benefits programs.

The Evolution of Enterprise Resource Software

Prior to the 1960s, if companies wanted to use their data, they typically would hire outside consultants to collate and analyze the data to provide information for decision making. In the 1960s, resource planning systems came into service when manufacturers saw the benefit of using computer systems to control inventory. During the next several decades, the systems evolved, first for material requirement planning and then for manufacturing resource planning.

Fast-forward to the 1990s, when enterprise resource planning (ERP) systems were no longer limited to manufacturing but also included human resources, finance, and project management functions. This allowed companies to manage core functions of the business that previously had been outsourced or managed by independent vendors.

Companies such as Oracle and SAP developed ERP systems to use one computer to integrate a company's key business functions for managing elements of the organization. ERP systems enable companies to bring together disparate data from different parts of the organization onto one platform and turn it into information, especially for the human resources, finance, and procurement functions. For the technology to be most effective, it needs to be scalable and adaptable so that as a company grows and adds new functionality, the platform is elastic enough to be able to meet those demands.

In addition to manufacturing, many other industries use ERP to improve their core business functions. For example, large retailers, such as Wal-Mart and Target, use ERP systems for managing their inventories and for ordering from their suppliers to assure that their shelves are quickly restocked on the basis of customers' purchases.

However, a key obstacle to leveraging the ERP system for health benefits is a lack of standardization in infrastructure and how information flows from one platform to another. Most companies haven't updated their legacy systems where information resides; other companies have homegrown systems that were built internally to capture business information. But the problem with these legacy systems is that information remains in silos. As companies grow or as they acquire other companies, these legacy systems also grow—but they still can't communicate with each other. One system handles payroll, another tracks lost time from work, another system monitors workers' compensation, and there's also a system for accounting. In most instances, data are not standardized, so they cannot move through the organization in a consistent flow. There may be a system for finance and a system for HR, but seldom is there one consistent platform that enables companies to have visibility into all of the finance information *and* all of the HR information. Companies should be able to manage their health benefits using the same platform that manages payroll, expenses, and time management functions.

The lack of standardization leads to a lack of transparency because constituents can't view the same data, and, of course, inefficiencies are the end result. Because information exists in discrete silos, companies don't have a comprehensive overview to use to make strategic health benefits decisions.

Transactional Data Are Not Enough

Systems are usually designed to capture a specific kind of transactional data, such as human resources systems capturing payroll data and benefits plan enrollment data. Medical claims data may be captured by a third-party vendor. The pharmacy data may be residing in another silo with a pharmacy benefits manager. Employee health risk assessment data could be sitting in an online Web portal and workers' compensation data in another HR system.

The transactional data we receive from our credit card companies show us how much money was spent during the previous month and where the money was spent.

Visa Signature Summary

Opening/Closing Date:
01/12/20XX

New Balance
$13,999.99

Payment Due Date:
02/01/20XX

9.1 Credit Card Statement with No Detail

Visa Signature Summary

Opening/Closing Date:
01/12/20XX

New Balance
$13,999.99

Payment Due Date:
02/01/20XX

TRANSACTIONS

Date	Description	Amount
12/02	U Save Groceries	$58.25
12/10	Gas and Go	$15.00
12/15	Sally's Deli	$7.58
12/20	Robert Smith, MD.	$125.57
12/20	Gas and Go	$12.00

9.2 Credit Card Statement with the Usual Detail

186

All of these systems need to be tied together to give companies a view into their total health-care costs. But if the data are residing in different legacy systems and not one common platform, it becomes a technological nightmare to bring all of the data together quickly so they can be analyzed and transformed into information that can be used to optimize health-care benefits.

Transactional data are simply not enough, especially when making decisions about health benefits. The transactional data we receive from our credit card companies show us how much money was spent during the previous month and where the money was spent. But imagine if the credit card statement provided comprehensive information on how much money was spent on specifics kinds of purchases or if it offered details on where to shop to get more value or, better yet, if it gave tips on how to trim monthly spending. That information would be more meaningful when deciding what to purchase in the next month.

Companies that receive only transactional data on their health-care spending aren't translating the data into information they can use to improve the cost and quality of their health benefits. Human resources managers just aren't receiving the kind of information that could help them make better decisions for managing health benefits by answering questions such as:

- How does employee plan selection help or hinder health and cost objectives?

- How does current employee health status relate to future health risk?

- Are employee cost shares equitable?

- Do contracted vendors help or hinder benefit strategies?

- Are excessive costs the result of faulty plan design?

187

- Do disease management and wellness programs achieve expected financial results?

- Are employees enrolled in the most appropriate plans for their health and financial needs?

Benefits accountants could also profit from receiving more than just transactional data on their company's health benefits. The finance department could make proactive decisions by being able to answers questions such as the following:

- How much do we need to allocate into the reserve for the next quarter?

- What is the impact of our benefits costs on profit margins?

- What is the level of ongoing duplicates or ineligible claims that require recovery?

- Is there any fraud or abuse in payments made against claims?

- Is there an opportunity to optimize the money set aside in reserve if we pay later instead of earlier?

Information, instead of data, could also help the finance department identify spending trends or improve forecasts for future benefits allocations. Information could also help finance when paying medical claims. The number of large companies that still reconcile their claims using spreadsheets on a daily or weekly basis is surprising. Each month, accounting departments need to reconcile all of the health benefits payments to the invoices sent by the insurance carriers to assure that payments and charges match, but, many times, the claims are paid without verifying the charges. These inefficiencies in the system are occurring because of the absence of one consistent platform on which the data can be systematized and then analyzed. Instead, analysis is performed on an ad hoc basis, which can result in errors. Even more detrimental, the data are not being captured for optimizing the health benefits plan design.

Transforming the Health-Care Industry

During the past several years, there has been a big push to incorporate information technology into the delivery of health care, such as electronic medical records and electronic prescribing for medications. In April 2004, President Bush signed Executive Order 13335—Incentives for the Use of Health Information Technology and Establishing the Position of the National Health Information Technology Coordinator. The order laid out the development and implementation of an interoperable health information technology to improve the quality and efficiency of health care.[1] The adoption of electronic medical records (EMRs) was a major part of the initiative.

The benefits of using EMRs include better-coordinated care for patients and cost savings that result from fewer errors and the waste that is inherent in a paper record system. However, despite the advantages to using EMRs, the economics of installing the high-tech systems prohibit some health-care providers and others in the health-care supply chain from adopting them.

Incentives are offered for some use of health information technology, such as the free ePrescribing software provided to the members of the National ePrescribing Patient Safety Initiative (NEPSI). But this is a small effort to solve a big problem. Many in the health-care industry recommend that the government play a more active role by providing incentives to help advance the use of EMRs. In 2008, the Health and Human Services Department announced a five-year Medicare pilot program to test the effectiveness of offering incentives to physicians for adopting electronic health records. Participants will receive increased Medicare payments for implementing the systems, using systems to report on their quality of care, and showing that they used the systems for meeting quality-of-care standards.[2]

EMRs will be beneficial to physicians' offices, and electronic prescribing will no doubt reduce the number of preventable medication errors, but those applications of health information technology won't help companies make better health-care purchasing decisions. Some business alliances and health-care organizations are developing their own Web-based systems to store medical records for their employees. Google and Microsoft have also provided individuals with the capability to store health information online.

A better use of the technology is to empower those who are spending the money to purchase health care. The current initiatives may minimize medical errors and improve patient safety, but the technology needs to be adopted across all of the constituents in the health-care supply chain to create one effective software platform. Speeding the transformation of the health-care industry will require the government to provide tax credits to enable companies to adopt such a platform. This would allow information to flow smoothly across the entire health-care supply chain.

Challenges of Integrating Information

Part of the challenge to creating a unified view of health benefits costs is that human resources practitioners don't have a deep understanding of health-care financing. In the past, HR managers were focused on providing the kinds of benefits that would attract a high-quality workforce. However, the traditional role of HR has changed dramatically because of the changing economic environment and the impact that health benefits have on a company's bottom line. Now, managing the HR function requires a fuller understanding of health care, finance, and technology previously not required to the same depth.

To gain this deeper, more well-rounded understanding of the full scope of health-care benefits, HR managers need to do the following things: (1) understand how to manage complex benefits strategies; (2) be able to measure the performance of benefit plans and compare vendor performance with corporate goals and objectives; (3) recognize how technology is the driving force behind making health-care decisions based on quality and cost; (4) gain insight into the metrics involved in the total cost of health care; and (5) understand how to quickly bring those metrics together, interpret them, and leverage the information in order to optimize benefits.

The lack of technology and the lack of understanding of the right metric can cause delays in decision making, adding to the cost of health care and further limiting a company's ability to control costs.

Until now, external consultants have been hired to help companies implement benefits strategies by making recommendations and providing estimates of the cost. Much of this work has to be performed manually, with consultants collecting medical claims data from the insurance carriers and pharmacy data from the pharmacy benefits manager and then crunching the numbers. Because this has been done on an ad hoc basis, the entire process is not only cumbersome and time-consuming but also expensive. It hasn't been easy for consulting companies either because they often have to put together teams of people to analyze the data and compile reports for use by the benefits department. This is a primary example of why companies haven't been able to effectively change their approach to health-care benefits to realize the kind of savings they expect.

INEFFICIENCIES IN THE PROCESS OF MANAGED DATA

▶ Delivering data on performance is not a core part of business for carriers

▶ Analytical qualities and detail are lost when carriers transform data using financial codes required for transactional processing

▶ No national standards for claim data formats

▶ Regulatory issues (HIPAA, confidentiality, etc.) slow down the process

▶ Employers require resources to fully analyze

▶ Data is often processed manually by consultants and this cost is often transferred back to employers

9.3   Inefficiencies in the Process of Managed Data

Transforming Data into Information

Technology eliminates the disconnect between finance and human resources by providing clear visibility into the total costs and risks related to health benefits. Technology allows the human resources group to be proactive instead of reactive in its benefits planning. Technology provides the human resources department with real-time information so trends can be identified, opportunities can be optimized, and benefits expenditures can be controlled throughout the entire health benefits management cycle.

Additionally, the finance department would be able to proactively manage the budget because it would no longer have to depend on a

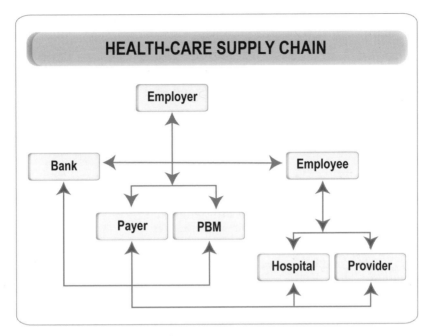

9.4   Health-Care Supply Chain

retrospective view of payments. These opportunities aren't possible using the current system because of the inefficiencies caused by information delays. When insurance carriers delay in sending invoice data, companies aren't able to close their books, reconcile, and budget in a timely manner. Ongoing delays cause a waterfall effect that results in further delays and an inability to budget effectively. Technology can help leverage those inefficiencies from an information standpoint and also can accelerate the time needed to make intelligent benefits decisions.

Delays in the flow of information create inefficiencies for all of the links in the supply chain. However, these inefficiencies provide opportunities for improving the delivery of information within the supply chain.

- From payer to employer, there are delays in data integrity, data format, and processing data.

- From payer to provider, there are delays in how claims are coded, processed, adjudicated, and paid.

- From provider to hospital, there are delays in how claims are coded, processed, adjudicated, and paid.

- From pharmacy benefits manager (PBM) to payer, there are delays in how claims are processed and paid and in how information about discounts is disseminated.

- From employer to employee, there are delays in enrollment data and information about benefits.

Technology Creates Healthy Solutions: DuPont

DuPont is the global multinational science company founded in 1802 and now operating in more than 70 countries. Dr. Wayne Lednar is DuPont's global chief medical officer and director of Integrated Health Services in Wilmington, Delaware. As DuPont's lead physician, Dr. Lednar helps ensure that the company has effective health programs for its workforce of 30,000 U.S. employees and 60,000 employees worldwide. He's also involved in assuring that the corporate health benefits program meets the needs of company groups, employees, family members, and retirees in locations around the world.

DuPont uses information technology systems to manage the health experiences of its workforce, from the hiring process through retirement. The company links information systems that traditionally haven't communicated with one another to help focus its resources on improving the cost and quality of health services. The goal is to keep employees healthy and productive at work.

Technology Helps Manage the Health Experience

Whenever an employee is not at work because of illness or injury, the cost of doing business increases because DuPont incurs the direct cost of medical care, as well as the indirect cost of short-term disability, lost productivity, or overtime for an experienced worker to fill the gap.

Integrated information systems help manage the health experience of DuPont's workforce and affect the bottom line by coordinating medical data with human resources systems. In addition to helping manage the general health of the workforce, technology organizes data from new-hire health examinations, manages data for personal health information, and coordinates workers' compensation, disability, and health plan claims data.

Preplacement Health Exams

Postoffer, preplacement health exams are necessary to assure a safe and effective job fit for the capabilities of a new employee and to identify potential health risks that would keep him or her from being safe and effective on the job. DuPont uses information technology to streamline its hiring process in order to

continues ▶

shorten the amount of time between job offer and beginning work. The sooner employees can get to work, the sooner they can become productive.

The medical support function uses technology for required regulated medical surveillance examinations. Data from medical instruments used for audiology tests, blood tests, and pulmonary function tests are fed directly into the system, eliminating the need for paper files or entering information into a computer system. In addition to providing job fit information, the data provide information about health conditions that aren't being managed or conditions that may need to be monitored to improve the overall health and productivity of the employee.

Personal Health Information

Information technology is used to manage personal health issues, whether due to illness or injury, by collecting and accurately storing data in a usable form. The technology is used to help assure that personnel policies are followed and that benefits, such as salary continuation, are administered as required. Keeping track of this information reduces the risk of noncompliance with federal or state employment regulations.

The Integrated Health Services group also uses technology to coordinate care and expedite medical appointments to help DuPont employees navigate the health-care system. Data provide clinical information to assure that timely diagnoses are made and that appropriate treatment plans are in place to help reduce the amount of medically related lost time. Data are used to ensure that employees are not being overtreated or undertreated, with the focus on helping employees get healthy and back to work as soon as possible while achieving greater patient understanding and engagement in their health and its management.

In addition to having portal access to a wide variety of Web-enabled health information sources, employees also have calculators and projection tools available to help them set health improvement goals and make health plan purchasing decisions that meet their life and family needs.

Workers' Compensation Claim Information

Because medical and legal forms are completed when a worker is injured on the job, technology is an effective way to integrate data from a number of internal and external sources. DuPont uses information systems to monitor the claims process and to eliminate the need for paper files. Increasingly, state authorities are requesting that employers utilize electronic data transfer in the reporting and adjudication of claims.

Reduced Costs, Improved Clinical Outcomes

DuPont uses technology to ensure that its workforce is healthy, safe, and effective at work. Reduced health-care costs are one result; the other is better clinical outcomes for DuPont employees. For the company, it is an effective workforce able to utilize its skills and talents to produce products for customers. Together, these form a competitive advantage.

Interpreting Data Has Clinical Applications

Another advantage to applying technology to health care is information interpretation. This means that when transactional data are combined, they will have more relevance than the data would alone. The number of times an individual visits a doctor or the diagnosis that results does not have as much impact as being able to combine data so that they become actionable information. Instead of looking at the number of physician visits, the kinds of lab tests, the diagnosis, and the medical procedure separately, technology provides the ability to combine all of these data together for a comprehensive picture of an individual's entire health-care episode. When data become actionable, companies can make health benefits decisions such as the kinds of physicians that need to be included in their networks.

Combining data in this manner provides information that can be used to determine risk. An individual with diabetes and high blood pressure may need an angioplasty performed in the future. Information such as this helps a company understand the likelihood—or risk—for a future cardiovascular procedure and the estimated resulting costs. Grouping clinical data and turning them into actionable information adds relevance to the data, just as the total health-care cost is more relevant than the direct medical costs alone. This can help a company and its employees make better health-care decisions.

Improved Technological Standards

Technology in and of itself won't improve health care or lower its costs; technology standards need to be implemented to assure information delivery, transparency, and integration. Standards should be consistent across industries so that information can be communicated from insurance carriers to companies, from carriers to physicians, and from physicians to employees. Just as in the banking system, consumers should be able to easily access their accounts for information. The challenge here is that insurance carriers all have different standards for how they transmit health-care data. Because of the number of different standards, companies have difficulties interpreting the data and transforming them into actionable information. Because of the many silos and different formats, there are potentially thousands of data combinations that companies are attempting to decode.

Because of the inefficiencies this causes, the drive to adopt health information technology is not surprising. However, three issues need to be addressed: (1) developing a plan for technology implementation, (2) creating incentives directed toward the right constituents to adopt the technology, and (3) installing infrastructure across the supply chain to transmit information.

The following diagram illustrates the supply chain and the technology that can be implemented by each link for more pervasive and accurate dissemination of information.

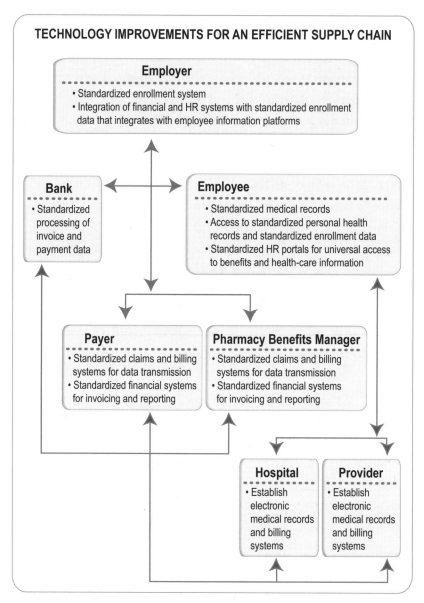

9.5   Technology Improvements for an Efficient Supply Chain

Health Information Technology Is the Competitive Edge—Intervoice

Intervoice is a company specializing in software-based interactive voice response (IVR) and contact center and mobile messaging technology. The company has headquarters in Dallas, Texas, and an international office in Manchester, England. About 650 employees and 2,000 dependents are covered by Intervoice's health benefits plan.

Under the direction of Don Brown, senior vice president for human resources and real estate, Intervoice has successfully leveraged its corporate information technology system to manage its health benefits program. In 2006, the company implemented an enterprise solution software to help find ways to reduce health-care costs by improving plan performance.

The medical program included three basic plans for its employees: high-deductible consumer-directed plans with a health savings account, a premium point-of-service (POS) insurance plan, and a standard POS plan.

Manual Operations Made Decisions Difficult

Prior to implementing the health benefits management software, the company had data residing in a number of internal and external systems. Human resources data, which included enrollment data and employee demographic data, resided on a system separate from the company's financial data; claims data resided with the insurance carrier. Because the data were

continues ▶

housed in several different systems, whenever the company needed information to make benefit plan changes, it required a labor-intensive manual process to compile data and input them into a spreadsheet for analysis.

Despite the large volume of data available to Intervoice, the company wasn't able to create information to use for making strategic decisions about the health benefits plan design, prescription benefits, or employee wellness programs.

Three Cost-Saving Approaches

The enterprise software solution sits on top of the company's SAP system to create a bridge between the data residing in human resources and financial systems and claims data residing in claims administrators' systems, allowing them to be easily sorted for analysis. Intervoice uses the system to monitor trends in health-care utilization and to make changes to its health benefits program. Because the applications can update and process in real time, Intervoice has used them for performing predictive modeling, analyzing utilization rates, and implementing targeted wellness programs.

Predictive Modeling

Intervoice used predictive modeling to balance employee cost shares by determining accurate and equitable plan rates and employee out-of-pocket costs. The company used 12 months of claims history to see how changes to the plan design would affect cost and the number of enrollees. Intervoice was able to determine that it could benefit by enrolling more employees in its high-deductible consumer-directed health plans if instead of charging a premium, it made monthly contributions from $600 to $1,200 to each participant's health savings account. Turning data into information also helped the company understand its return on investment for implementing this kind of plan design.

Implementing Targeted Wellness Programs

The technology also enabled Intervoice to conduct a utilization analysis of its prescription drug spending. The analysis provided information on how much money was being spent on prescription drugs and which of the more expensive drugs had the highest utilization rates. This data gave the company insight into the kinds of changes it could make to its prescription drug benefit to reduce costs without sacrificing health-care quality.

In addition, when trends showed a rise in costs associated with prescription drugs used to manage certain health conditions, such as high blood pressure or high cholesterol, the company implemented "heart healthy" programs to increase awareness and monitor the conditions. One example was a free program for employees and their spouses to have their blood pressures and cholesterol levels checked on a regular basis.

continues ▶

Communicating with Employees

Intervoice has a company-wide focus on employee wellness, and new health improvement and education programs are designed to target specific populations based on utilization and claims data. Multiple communication channels are used to provide information, including e-mail, newsletters, and meetings. The company also hosts a large health fair annually.

Part of the company's success in managing its health-care costs has been educating employees on the benefits of the consumer-directed health plans and the ways that they can help keep claims costs down. In one instance, utilization data showed an increase in the number of people using the services of a hospital emergency room. Because this is a more costly option for care than seeing a primary-care physician during office hours or visiting an urgent-care center, the company addressed the issue with employees through a communications campaign. Intervoice was able to communicate to employees the benefits of using urgent care or taking care of problems before they required an ER visit. A nurse hotline was also implemented to help drive costs down.

Intervoice understands that some health events may always be unforeseen, but the benefits management software helps the company monitor the median of the claims because that is where change can have the most impact.

A One-Year ROI

Intervoice found that the ROI for implementing the health benefits management software occurred during its first year of use. The company has not increased health premiums or plan costs for three consecutive years. In addition to providing information for improving the health plan design and implementing special programs to manage costs, the system flags double payments that might not have been caught in the past.

Intervoice updates its data frequently to monitor health benefits status and to plan for the future. The company credits its health plan for helping to recruit and retain its talented staff in a competitive market. Employees say that the number-one reason they stay at Intervoice is the depth and breadth of the benefits offering.

Chapter 9—Key Messages

- Companies have invested millions of dollars in technology to run their internal operations, yet they aren't leveraging the technology to improve the cost and quality of their health benefits.

- Technology is a critical component for any health benefits strategy because it helps companies make informed, exacting decisions based on real-time information.

continues ▶

- Linking financial and human resources data streamlines efficiency and transparency throughout the entire health benefits supply chain.

- Effectively managing a health-care benefits program is so complex that HR practitioners need insight into the total cost of health care in order to optimize benefits.

- Technology improves vendor performance, claims validation, billing and remittance, and approvals processes.

- Health information technology, in the form of electronic medical records and e-prescribing, will help improve patient care, but a better use of the technology is empowering those who are spending the money to purchase health care.

Chapter 9—Endnotes

1   "Executive Order 13335—Incentives for the Use of Health Information Technology and Establishing the Position of the National Health Information Technology Coordinator," *Federal Register*, April 30, 2004, 2004 Executive Orders Disposition Tables, http://www.archives.gov/federal-register/executive-orders/2004.html.

2   U.S. Department of Health and Human Services, "Electronic Health Records Advancing 21st Century Medicine: New Medicare Demonstration Project to Provide Incentives for Using EHRs to Improve Quality of Care," http://www.hhs.gov/news/facts/20080131c.html.

CHAPTER 10

COMMUNICATION ISSUES

> *"Great spirits have always found violent opposition from mediocre minds."*
>
> —Albert Einstein

During the past several years, companies have made progress in understanding how to use the metrics of cost, utilization, and risk for purchasing health care. However, they have one more opportunity to drive health-care change, and that is through helping employees become better consumers of health care with targeted communications. This is a win-win for companies and their employees. Companies benefit from targeted marketing efforts because they help employees become actively engaged in their health care, and employees benefit from having the kind of information they need to become informed health-care consumers.

Communication efforts haven't been as effective at driving change as companies have expected for a number of reasons. One reason is that most companies haven't spent the required amount of time to establish themselves as credible sources of information. Some companies leave it to their insurance carriers to communicate directly with employees throughout the year. That leaves companies to communicate with employees about health benefits only during open enrollment. In addition to a lack of consistent communication, the communication hasn't been personalized. While sending out a flier on the first day of summer with skin cancer reminders and packets of sunscreen is a good idea, this type of generic communication isn't enough.

Employees have become better health-care consumers on their own because of the push toward consumer-directed plans and tiered networks. Restructured health benefits empower employees to take charge of the spending for their health care. However, the cost of health care is not transparent because companies absorb most of the cost. This is different from other aspects of the economy where consumers are used to knowing the price of goods and services and can adjust their consumption accordingly. When the price of gasoline exceeded $4.00 per gallon in 2008, consumers made changes to their driving habits. They drove slower, drove fewer miles, and relied more on public transportation. They also adjusted their other spending habits, cutting back on nonessential goods and services to meet the demands of rising gas prices.

That is just one example of how consumption is directly affected by a drastic change in prices. However, in health care, changing price doesn't necessarily have a direct impact on consumption because people are reluctant to compromise when it comes to their health—and understandably so. Health isn't perceived as a commodity, so consumers don't feel that health care should be restricted on the basis of price sensitivity in the market, but the highest-quality health care should be provided at any cost. This presumption doesn't exist in other areas of the free market. Because employer-sponsored health-care plans have contributed to the idea of entitlement, making downward adjustments in either cost or quality has been difficult.

Companies should be able to entrust their employees to take greater responsibility for their health care to help drive efficiency within the system. They can help empower employees to make informed decisions about their health-care choices with more effective communication.

Changing the Health-Care Ecosystem—Dr. Paul Grundy

Paul Grundy, MD, MPH, is an advocate for patient-centered primary care in his dual roles as director of health-care transformation for IBM and chairman of the Patient-Centered Primary Care Collaborative. His goal is to transform health care by creating partnerships between the purchasers of health care and the primary-care providers.

IBM spends about $2 billion annually on health care for its employees. The company has created robust prevention and wellness programs that have helped it realize significant health-care savings, but these initiatives are the low-hanging fruit of health-care improvement. Companies that want to have a real impact on health-care cost and quality need to address the fundamental issues of why health care in the United States is so expensive but offers so little value to its consumers.

To change the health-care ecosystem, companies need to work together with their insurance carriers and networks of primary-care physicians to develop a system of integrated, comprehensive, coordinated care. This approach emphasizes the importance of each employee developing a relationship with his or her primary-care physician. Studies show that when individuals can identify a PCP by name, health-care costs go down and mortality rates also decline.

However, many employees in companies across the country don't get the preventive services and screening tests that would find health problems such as breast cancer and colon cancer while they are still treatable. For real change to occur, employers need to look at the broader issue of health care and choose to focus more on robust primary care and prevention services. Instead of buying episodes of care, employers should be paying the providers for delivering comprehensive integrated care.

continues ▶

Communicating with Employees

IBM is at the forefront of innovative efforts to reduce health-care spending trends by encouraging employees to become more engaged in their health care and developing closer relationships with their primary-care doctors. Health-care messages tend to stick when physicians communicate them and when the company provides rewards for following them.

IBM's health benefit structure includes a plan choice with no health-care premiums for employees, cash rebates for positive health behaviors, fully paid preventive care, and low-cost primary care without deductibles. Online quality information is provided for employees to help in making health-care decisions, with cash rewards for reviewing quality data.

IBM is focused on a problem that inhibits the development of a truly patient-centered model of real, meaningful care. One of IBM's recommendations is to create a reimbursement structure that rewards providers primarily for increasing patient health instead of for seeing as many patients as possible, as is the case today.

The company's communication efforts provide an open dialogue with employees about why IBM is working to have better prevention with no co-pays and no deductibles. IBM is driving a transformation of health care where employees are empowered to develop a relationship with their PCPs and to communicate directly with their doctors by using tools such as e-mail to ask questions.

A wide range of health resources are provided, including personal physicians, "one-stop shopping" for health care, telephone advice lines, healthy living programs, and online health and wellness tools.

Communicating with Employers

Large self-insured employers such as IBM are working together with primary-care physicians and health insurance companies to change the way health care is purchased. The Patient-Centered Primary Care Collaborative (http://www.PCPCC.net) is a coalition of major employers, consumer groups, and others who have joined with organizations representing primary-care physicians to develop and advance the patient-centered medical home model of primary care.

The group worked together to develop guidelines and a *Patient-Centered Medical Home Purchaser Guide* to communicate ways for taking action. The goal is to change the way health care is delivered by making primary-care physicians more accessible, promoting prevention, and engaging patients in managing their health conditions.

Together, the collaborative is addressing the issue of how to provide comprehensive, continuous, patient-centered primary care based on a relationship between patients and their physicians.

Consumerism Is Driven by Information

Advertising is big business for a good reason—it engages consumers of all ages who want to make good purchasing decisions. Advertisements are targeted to meet the needs of certain demographics, whether teenagers, senior citizens, or young adults. Health-care consumers have different needs, too, so it's no surprise that a one-size-fits-all communications approach won't be as effective as a targeted approach. The three "I" words companies can use when thinking about ways to attract the attention of health-care consumers are incentives, information, and infrastructure.

Incentives are necessary to provide a motivating environment for employees to take on the health-care-consumer role. Plan design and cost-sharing features, such as premium contributions, coinsurance, deductibles, and drug formularies, must be optimized. Effective reward systems should be designed to motivate desirable lifestyle behaviors.

Information in the form of personal health content, promotions, and analytics builds awareness. Employees must have ready access to information as health issues arise, as well as resources for healthy living and smart, proactive health-care purchasing. Companies also need to consider change management concepts so employees are aware of the rationale behind health-care initiatives.

Infrastructure is the foundation for implementing and supporting program objectives and includes a combination of health advisory

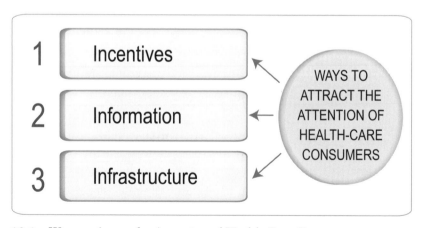

10.1   Ways to Attact the Attention of Health-Care Consumers

information, data, and technology. Consolidated programs for health and wellness, disease management, and counseling must be integrated with online decision support and empowerment tools. Employees and their significant others and dependents should all be fully engaged for the initiatives to be successful.

For employees to become engaged as health-care consumers, technology and communication must be linked. The more technology a

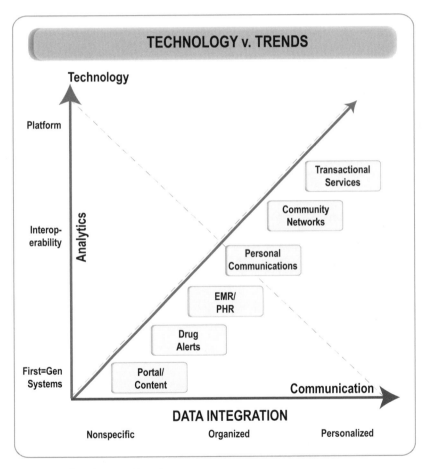

10.2   Technology v. Trends

company adopts for communicating with its employees on health-care issues, the more effective the communication becomes. Companies may begin with Web portals using first-generation systems, but the more interoperability that is implemented, the more sophisticated communications can become. This moves communication from content-only information to information that alerts consumers about prescription medications, supports access to personal health records, connects with community networks, and provides transactional services.

Six Segments of Health-Care Consumers

In 2008, the Deloitte Center for Health Solutions, part of Deloitte LLP, conducted an online survey of health-care consumers. The results showed that consumers want more from the health-care system, including more access to their health-care providers, online access to their medical records, and the chance to customize their insurance coverage.[1] In addition, the survey identified a profile of six health-care-consumer segments, their preferences regarding care, how much they depended on their providers for information, the degree with which they complied with treatment, how satisfied they were with their providers and plans, and other differentiators. The six descriptive classifications and the percentage of individuals who identified themselves in each segment included the following:

- Content and Compliant (28%)
- Casual and Cautious (28%)
- Sick and Savvy (24%)
- Online and Onboard (8%)

- Out and About (9%)

- Shop and Save (2%)

The results of this survey, and others like it, can be used by companies to implement consumer-driven health plans that respond to each segment's health-care preferences and to personalize their communication efforts to each segment. For example, some health-care consumers aren't interested in shopping for insurance, while others are interested in receiving information about health-care quality and would like to customize their insurance. One segment prefers more access to online tools, but another is more interested in cost and is less likely to use special services.

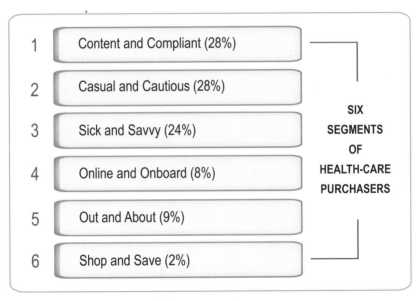

1   Content and Compliant (28%)

2   Casual and Cautious (28%)

3   Sick and Savvy (24%)

4   Online and Onboard (8%)

5   Out and About (9%)

6   Shop and Save (2%)

SIX SEGMENTS OF HEALTH-CARE PURCHASERS

10.3   Six Segments of Health-Care Purchasers

How to Engage Consumers

From an informational standpoint, many periodicals, Web sites, and programs have been developed to educate consumers on how to manage their health. While this information is helpful, it is generally not engaging enough to keep consumers returning to get information on which to base their health-care decisions. Companies can transform employees into engaged health-care consumers in the following four ways:

1. Create branded marketing initiatives that focus on health information messages to drive awareness and affect attitude.

2. Design individualized experiences that engage employees to return for more information.

3. Encourage trust to enable a free flow of information.

4. Use a system of rewards to drive consistent outcomes.

To be successful at engaging consumers, companies need to implement the principles of trust, transparency, targeted marketing, personalized information, a variety of services, incentives, the necessary tools, and a sense of community.

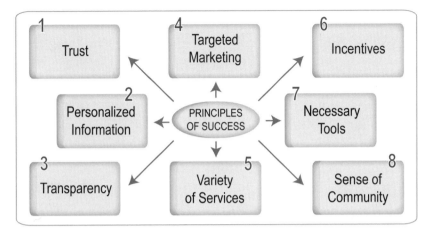

10.4   **Principles of Success**

Build Trust

Consumers have always needed a trusted source for information because trust allows for a free flow of information, something critical to engaging employees as consumers. For many years, Walter Cronkite was the gold standard for trust in the news—back when there were only three broadcast television channels. Now consumers have many more individuals whom they trust for information, depending on their individual preferences, from personality to whether their trusted source agrees with their principles, values, or politics.

In the past, consumers received information about their health care from their health plans, but companies should fill the role of the trusted source for information to empower health-care consumers. Companies can develop this trust by (1) emphasizing the quality of care over the cost of care and (2) addressing the issue of privacy and assuring the confidentiality of information.

Companies should also be aware that the need for individual privacy is evolving. Consider that only ten years ago, most of us didn't feel comfortable making credit card purchases online. Now many people conduct much of their shopping and banking transactions online. In time, consumers will feel comfortable providing that same level of health-care information online in order to receive the same amount of efficiency. This is especially true if health-care consumers know that they can trust their source of information and that their information is completely secure.

Ensure Transparency

Consumers want to know how their efforts are affecting the cost and quality of health care; however, the lack of transparency into this information is a barrier. Companies need to make it easy for employees to gain visibility into the cost of care and the performance of the physicians in their health-care plans to enable them to make better-quality health-care decisions.

Additionally, consumers want to see measurable results for how their behavior has an impact—either in dollars saved or in improved outcomes. For example, if employees sign up for a company-sponsored smoking cessation program, they understand that they are reducing their risk for heart disease or lung cancer. But they haven't been shown quantitatively how they have reduced their expected health-care utilization or the resulting savings by quitting now instead of quitting five years from now. Information transparency such as this helps consumers tie their behavior to the impact it has on the cost and quality of outcomes that will help drive meaningful change.

Target the Health-Care Decision Makers

Companies that want to improve their communications with health-care consumers need to target the individual who makes the health-care decisions. In almost two-thirds of the country's households, women are responsible for making health-care decisions for their families; more than 80 percent of women have either sole or shared responsibility for making the financial decisions for their families' health.[2] This means that companies need to work to communicate with the female member of the employee's household, whether the employee, the spouse, or the significant other.

That communication needs to be targeted, but it also needs to be engaging. Communications need to keep the decision maker actively involved in the management of the family's health and include information that is relevant to all of the members of the household, from infants, toddlers, and teens to perhaps even the most senior residents.

Personalize Information

Communication needs to contain information that is personalized because a one-size-fits-all approach doesn't work. The information needs to be relevant, engaging, and consistent. Unfortunately, health care has yet to become as sophisticated as other consumer markets that have an overwhelming amount of market research and trend analysis.

Until health care catches up, it can take lessons from other successful consumer models. Consider the kind of experience consumers have when dealing with online retailers, especially Amazon.com. This company is skilled at personalizing consumers' experiences by alerting customers to information that is relevant to them, such as book titles, music CDs, or movie DVDs, based on previous purchases. This engages the consumers and keeps them returning to the site because all of their information is stored there and purchases are processed quickly. Health-care communication should be similar in engaging consumers and having them return for information.

Most health-related sites, such as the American Diabetes Association or the American Cancer Society, provide somewhat generic information on symptoms and treatment options. To be most effective, consumers would benefit from personalized information on the most practical treatment approach relevant to their history.

Here are two scenarios that illustrate the difference that personalized information can have on someone with a chronic health condition.

Scenario 1

An individual with diabetes and high blood pressure wants to learn more about these two diseases and the resulting complications. He searches the Internet looking for information and finds several articles about the two conditions. But this information doesn't specifically address a family history of diabetes and a history of glaucoma, too. The medication the individual is currently prescribed isn't listed as a treatment therapy. In conjunction with the Internet search, the individual has contacted the insurance carrier and requested information. A packet of generic diabetes educational materials was sent through the mail.

Scenario 2

An individual with diabetes and high blood pressure wants to learn more about these two diseases and the resulting complications. He goes to the company's Web site to look for information and completes a health risk assessment and opts in to receive information about the benefits covered in the employer-sponsored health plan. The individual is able to get a claims history on what has been spent on physician visits and prescription medications and views specific program information on diabetes and hypertension. This includes a list of possible side effects from the individual's medication and contact information for a nurse coordinator who the individual can call or e-mail for information on managing diabetes with the complicating factor of high blood pressure. The individual receives information on a rewards program that gives discounts on medications and monitoring equipment for participating in a diabetes coaching program.

In scenario 1, a lack of personalized information results in a lack of individual engagement. In scenario 2, the individual is actively engaged in managing his health care.

Provide a Variety of Services

Companies that offer consumer-directed health plans should empower their employees with the resources to provide information to help them manage their health savings accounts. Communications that provide information on services that engage employees on a regular basis can lead to informed, proactive health-care choices. Services could include computer alerts to remind individuals with asthma when pollen counts are high or other preventive care reminders. Services such as this are relevant and provide health reminders that might not otherwise be available.

Companies can also act as a clearinghouse for information that may be provided by their vendors, such as the insurance carrier, the pharmacy benefits manager, or the disease management company, so employees aren't overwhelmed with communications or messages that might be contradictory.

In addition, consumers need to be linked to their providers as a way to manage their care. For example, some companies provide services such as a nurse helpline or an onsite wellness center that serves employees, spouses, and dependents. These centers treat minor health complaints and provide flexible scheduling. Companies have found that providing facilities for care onsite minimizes the direct cost of medical care and reduces some indirect costs such as lost time from work.

One example of a company's successful efforts to control health insurance costs is ScottsMiracle-Gro. The Scotts Wellness Center in Marysville, Ohio, is a state-of-the-art wellness center that includes a medical office, fitness center, and pharmacy.[3] Incentives are offered to employees to use the facility and participate in health assessments. In return, they receive low-cost co-payments, free access to health coaches, free generic prescription drugs, and lowered health insurance premiums.[4] To demonstrate its commitment to its Live Total health program, the company is a tobacco-free employer.

Several studies have examined the return on investment that companies have achieved by investing in corporate wellness or health management programs. This doesn't factor in the potential returns

---

Return on Investment (ROI) is a financial measure.

- Can be estimated prospectively or retrospectively

What is ROI?

- How much you (expect to) save, compared with how much you (expect to) spend or have spent
- Expressed as a ratio (e.g., 2:1)
- ROI and savings are not the same:
  - Savings reflect differences in $ with vs. without the intervention
  - ROI = Savings / program costs, in today's dollars
  - NPV = Savings minus program costs, in today's dollars
  - ROI can be low but savings can be high

10.5 Cost-Benefit Primer

enabled by more targeted messaging or the use of technology to better engage consumers.

The successful measurement and ROI includes a detailed economic evaluation of the potential saving that can be obtained. There are specific methodologies for evaluating the return on investment for programs that enable the corporation to determine whether the investment in a wellness program has any economic benefits.

Offer Incentives

Health-care consumers need encouragement and positive reinforcement for making healthy choices, especially for managing the chronic conditions that have the most impact on health and that drive health-care costs: diabetes, hypertension, low-back pain, and asthma.

Many companies have had success offering incentive or award programs as positive reinforcement, including cash contributions, free fitness center memberships, or discounts on products or pharmacy medications. To be most effective, incentives need to be tied to outcomes so their impact can be measured.

Implement the Necessary Tools

For many companies, claims data on health-care services are the only information they have about the health-care histories of their employee population. To add to their knowledge base, some companies have implemented health risk assessments to help understand some of their employees' risk factors that might not be apparent from the claims data, such as smoking history, high blood pressure, or family health risk factors. An important part of getting employees to complete these assessments is providing rewards or incentives, such as reduced premiums and co-payments.

To be most beneficial, the health risk assessment data need to be integrated with the claims data to give insight into the kinds of programs that would best meet the health-care needs of employees. Aggregated data such as these are what help drive personalization and can help make an impact on the health of the employee population.

Companies are also communicating the benefits to employees for completing online personal health records. These efforts empower employees as consumers to take control of managing their health information, using a common technology platform to do so. One benefit is that online tools such as these help connect employees directly to their providers. Personal health records can be used to access and collate information from their medical records. Many health plans are pushing their network of physicians to provide online access to an integrated medical record that provides information from office visits, lab tests, and hospital stays.

Another option is being able to communicate with physicians through e-mail, and, in some instances, consumers are willing to pay for this service if it's available to them. This nontraditional approach to communicating with physicians via e-mail is another way to connect consumers directly with their providers.

One important aspect of online personal health records is that companies need to assure that the information is portable. Once employees' health information is consolidated, they should be assured that it's kept in a record that will always be available to them. The challenge with online personal health information is that consumers will have to understand the value of electronic medical records and the benefits of being able to access their medical information online. This provides an additional opportunity for companies to fill the role of a trusted resource.

Build a Sense of Community

Another means of keeping consumers engaged is building community by using Internet and intranet resources. Many individuals with chronic health conditions, or those who have been recently diagnosed with an illness, are interested in sharing experiences with others who have similar conditions to learn about treatment options, medication side effects, and an expected prognosis. These communities started with disease-specific nonprofit organizations and have moved to other sites on the Internet.

In addition to gaining information and having the opportunity to provide emotional support, consumers also benefit from word-of-mouth referrals that happen through social-networking sites. It will become equally important for companies to help their employees build a sense of community, too. One way is to create new portals and new platforms that are available for consumers to store their electronic health records and to have this information linked to the benefits information. This would provide another opportunity for consumers to become engaged in managing their health care and would help them make better health-care-spending decisions.

Chapter 10—Key Messages

- Companies that want to engage their employees as consumers need to create branded marketing of health information, design personalized communication for consumers, build trust to allow for a free flow of information, and use rewards to drive consistent outcomes.

continues ▶

- To become a credible source of information, companies need to work harder to become transparent in the cost and quality of health care.

- An effective platform for consumer engagement includes incentives, information, and infrastructure.

- For companies to see the most return on their communication efforts, they need to become more sophisticated in using technology to communicate with their consumer audience.

Chapter 10—Endnotes

1   Deloitte Center for Health Solutions, Deloitte LLP, *Deloitte's 2008 Survey of Health Care Consumers*, "Many U.S. Consumers Want Major Changes in Health Care Design, Delivery," http://www.deloitte.com.

2   U.S. Department of Health and Human Services, Office on Women's Health, "Women's Health Issues: An Overview," May 2000, http://www.womenshealth.org/owh/pub/womhealth%20issues/index.htm.

3   ScottsMiracle-Gro Company, "Corporate Responsibility Report 2006," http://thescottsmiraclegrocompany.com/en_US/pdf_docs/2006%20Corp%20Resp.pdf.

4   M. Thompson, "Benefit or Burden—Scotts Aggressively Attacks Rising Health Insurance Costs," WOSU NPR NewsRoom, Oct. 15, 2007, http://www.publicbroadcasting.net/wosu/news.newsmain?action=article&ARTICLE_ID=1164577.

BUILDING SOCIAL NETWORKS

"Every patient carries her or his own doctor inside."

—Albert Schweitzer

The World Wide Web has evolved during the past several years from a static read-and-respond approach for gaining information into a second stage of dynamic Internet-based services called Web 2.0. Now individuals no longer just get information from visiting Web sites; they can also interact in the same Web space with one another through social-networking sites such as Facebook and MySpace. Just as the technology has evolved to facilitate social networking, social networking has also evolved. Individuals now feel comfortable using social-networking sites to share information about their personal health experiences.

The concept of developing social networks around health-care topics isn't new. In the 1980s, professional online networks, or list-servs, were used by physicians and researchers to communicate with each other to exchange information on current research, research results, and treatment guidelines. As a practicing ophthalmologist, I used these information exchanges to learn the newest standards and to focus on difficult ophthalmology cases, such as treating a complicated case of optic neuritis. While the idea of using social networks to gain health-care information isn't new from a provider's perspective, what is new is the idea of developing specialized interactive online communities for consumers. Some innovative approaches include using virtual computer worlds for promoting healthy lifestyles and creating virtual health fairs. Approaches such as these are far removed from the early e-mail discussion groups that focused on a specific health condition.

Web 2.0 has also facilitated the push for consumers to take more control of their health information by using online tools for creating personal health records and completing online health risk assessments. Google Health and Microsoft's HealthVault platforms allow individuals to compile their health information online so it can be shared with their health-care providers.

According to recent research, the majority of computer users—some estimates are as high as 75 percent of users—turn to the Internet for health and medical information.[1] With this level of participation by "e-patients" and the trend toward social networking, building interactive health-care social networks is inevitable and will be an integral part of health care in the future: Health 2.0.

Social Networking and Health Care

The phenomenon of social networking has resulted in millions of people socializing on Web sites for developing friendships and business relationships, as well as sharing blogs, wikis, photos, and videos. As these personal uses evolve into sharing health-care experiences, there are eight key points to keep in mind.

Information Windows Have Closed

New health-focused social networks, search engines, and content distributors have made it easier for individuals to access the same information at the same time. That means that the health-care industry needs to educate consumers at the same time that it educates physicians. Consumers now have access to information that was once privileged only to the industry. Social computing makes it possible for almost anyone to quickly arm him- or herself with information, ask more questions, and take charge of personal health decisions.

Many advocacy groups and government agencies are taking advantage of this approach and offering their own specialized communication with consumers. Web sites can provide interaction with individuals, such as sending alerts and reminders through e-mail accounts and wireless mobile devices. Organizations such as the American Cancer

Society and the Centers for Disease Prevention have experimented with Second Life, the popular online three-dimensional site, to test whether social networks can be used to communicate important health information. Individuals participating in virtual communities have the potential to connect with one another in a completely different format.

Collaboration Makes Us Smarter

Now that it's faster and easier for health groups, physicians, health organizations, and consumers to connect and collaborate, people are learning about new treatments, alternative solutions, and less expensive options. Collaborations are helping diverse groups approach complicated health issues together and in a systematic manner.

Millions of Americans use the Internet on a daily basis to search for health information and to have conversations with others, building e-communities around specific conditions. Social networks, built on blinded information, are helping government agencies and pharmaceutical companies with their research. The challenge to collaborations such as these is how to assure that privacy guidelines are followed and how to address the potential for conflicts of interest.

Direct Dialogues Are Possible

For the most part, the health-care industry has been based on the "few-to-many" approach to communications, marketing, and product development. Technology has made it possible for the industry to connect with all of its constituencies in a more personalized and relevant way. These new direct links with consumer patients, for example, could mean better product design, new treatments, more effective trials, and, ultimately, more personalized health solutions instead of generic health information. Online health profiles provide the opportunity for health-care providers to communicate directly with their patients, wherever they may be, because cell phones and mobile technology make communication instantaneous.

Transparency Is a Requirement

People want information on the companies providing their health care, and social networks are lifting the veil on the traditionally complex and closed industry. Social networks are creating savvy consumers who want to communicate with their health-care providers in more transparent ways.

For this to occur, entities throughout the health-care supply chain need to leverage technology and standardize the exchange of information to create the kind of transparency that consumers need in order to drive better outcomes. The Health 2.0 platform can empower consumers with the ability to get the information they need to gain that transparency for making health-care decisions.

Similarly, if companies also have the same level of transparency into health-care economics, then the entire health-care supply chain will benefit. Once the platform that drives transparency is connected to where the dollars originate, then companies and their employees will be the beneficiaries.

Social Networks Create Marketing Opportunities

Word-of-mouth marketing has always been an important way that friends and family members share information about health care. Now, via social networks, health-care information is shared with a larger group of online friends, whether for staying informed on medical developments, learning about physician ratings, or researching treatment options for managing a specific illness.

From a business perspective, this opens opportunities for the health-care industry to rethink how it focuses its marketing efforts and leverages word-of-mouth marketing in a hyper-connected world. For example, individual health profiles can be used to create targeted advertising messages to groups of individuals, especially younger Internet users who are accustomed to sharing personal details through their Facebook and MySpace pages.

Knowledge Now Lives Forever

Web 2.0 technologies assure that community-driven knowledge will become more meaningful. Archived information, shared wisdom, and personal experience will have much longer life spans than ever before.

Costs Are Driven Down

Education and collaboration will force the industry to find innovative ways to keep costs down. People will have improved access to affordable health care because they will be able to easily locate new solutions and alternative options.

Privacy Replaced by a Culture of Collaborative Action

Despite the fact that health issues are considered private, online message boards, blogs, and social-networking sites are full of personal health information. This open sharing of information empowers consumers and leads them to make better choices about what they will and will not share. This new culture of openness will require additional protections, but consumers will benefit from being able to tap into a large and collaborative base of knowledge and experience.

For example, Web sites such as dailystrength.org provide online health support for individuals interested in learning about research, treatments, and alternative therapies. Thanks to Web 2.0 technologies, millions of individuals are able to openly connect with others to develop virtual communities, not just for emotional support but also for clinical knowledge. This approach is a powerful way to keep consumers engaged in their health care.

The challenge in building these kinds of communities within the work environment deals with privacy issues. But employees could be directed to social-networking sites outside the work environment, which would alleviate these privacy concerns.

Health 2.0 Is Patient Centered

Health 2.0 is not about consumer-directed health care; it's about patient-empowered health care. Patients should have the information they need to make rational health-care decisions because transparency of information is based on outcomes, not price. In the Health 2.0 paradigm, every link in the health-care supply chain is focused on increasing value for the *individual with illness*.

Health 2.0 is a new concept of health care where consumers, employers, payers, and physicians focus on improving outcomes. Social networking is a means to promote collaboration and communication between all of those constituents.

Health 2.0 relies on the interoperability of all health information: personal health records (PHRs), clinical health records (CHRs), enterprise health records (EHRs), and the national health record (NHR). All of the records must be based on standards that allow a seamless transmission between environments, with established security and privacy protocols in place. In addition, health information needs to be easy to access, anytime and from anywhere.

The mobility of information will speed the use of online content, and cloud computing will help make this happen. Cloud computing is when applications and data storage are managed by remote servers on high-speed networks instead of by a hosted center with a designated machine. The advantage to cloud computing is that it provides the opportunity for increased patient access because information can be sent to cell phones and mobile devices. But this is a problem for health applications where the provenance and security of medical records is a special concern. We're accustomed to having firewalls that protect medical data from others who might misuse them. Transparency between individuals and cloud vendors will be critical to how health information technology is tied to cloud computing in the future.

Web 2.0 for health care is built on the four cornerstones that form the foundation for the value-driven health-care movement: connectivity, price, quality, and incentives. These four components create a virtuous cycle of innovation and reform. Transparency serves as the catalyst for this process by creating positive change that can deliver better outcomes at a lower cost. As more information becomes available as a result of increased transparency, a wave of innovation will flow from all points along the full cycle of care, including phases where health-care service providers educate, prevent, diagnose, prepare, intervene, recover, monitor, and manage the various disease states. Measuring someone's glycosolated hemoglobin testing (HgA1c) does not accurately reflect the effectiveness of diabetic treatments; measuring ejection fraction (Ef) isn't an accurate reflection of the effectiveness of cardiovascular treatments. The care provided over the full cycle needs to be factored in to appropriately determine value.

An increased amount of personal health and outcome information will create an ongoing role for infomediaries and related service providers to add value at each stage of the full cycle of care. This value-added information can be sourced by hundreds of companies, in thousands of forms, to millions of people who can benefit from the remixing of medically related information. It is easy to see how the new Web 2.0 framework, with its inherent social-networking and collaboration tools on one integrated platform, will change health-care communication.

The platform of the future is one that will be ideal for supporting a social network for health care because employees will be on the same platform as their employers. The platform includes a data warehouse that stores data from employee health risk assessments, medical benefits information, pharmacy benefits information, enrollment, workers' compensation, and lab results. These data are supported by an analytical

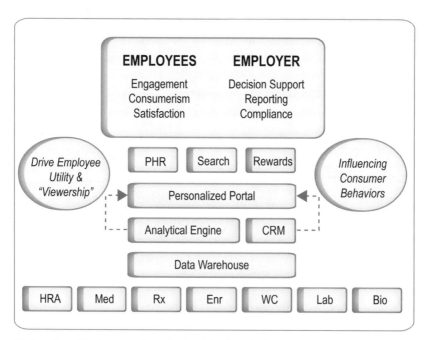

11.1   One Platform to Revolutionize Health-Care

engine that supports the employees' personalized portal. Employees can use the portal to compile their personal health records, search for information, and receive rewards based on their participation. Employees benefit from a network such as this through increased engagement and consumerism, leading to increased satisfaction. Employers benefit from a system that provides comprehensive reports, assures compliance, and can be used for making health benefits decisions.

A Model for Health 2.0

Health 2.0 relies on interoperability so individuals can share their personalized health information across the health-care supply chain. The ideal platform has an adaptable technology platform so that all constituents can drive information to or extract information from other links

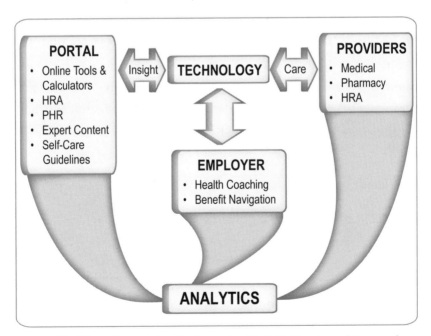

11.2   The Next-Generation Platform for Health-Care Social Networks

in the supply chain, such as insurance carriers, physicians, pharmaceutical companies, labs, and pharmacy benefits managers. The ability to bring in information from all of these areas into one technology platform is a fundamental concept.

A second fundamental concept is the need for an analytical layer to integrate all of the data and translate them into actionable information. This requires an additional engine that takes the actionable information and personalizes it for the employee. Personalization occurs through the profiles of the transactional and self-reported data so that they are pushed to the consumers to keep them engaged and returning to the portal for information. In addition, a feedback loop should monitor the interactions within the system to measure and evaluate how information is being optimized.

That level of feedback can create a platform of efficiency within Health 2.0. However, if the technology isn't aligned with the economics of health care, it becomes nothing more than a social science experiment because no real efficiencies can be derived from that. For Health 2.0 to be most successful, technology needs to enable more efficient dissemination of information and transparency of information across all constituents in order to enable more effective purchasing through visibility and the metrics of cost and quality.

A Vision for an Enterprise-Wide System

Companies need to develop a blueprint for creating an enterprise-wide platform that includes all of the key metrics needed to support the organization's initiatives. The metrics are those that show the affect of health risk on financial risk.

This blueprint will serve as the framework for how technology and investments in technology should be aligned for the entire organization to be able to integrate human resources, procurement, and finance with other key constituents across the company. This would ensure that those metrics are clearly visible and that they have the breadth and depth of information necessary to make the right decision in a timely manner.

In an ideal world, integrating systems requires being able to effectively receive data from every vendor, including medical insurance carriers, dental and vision insurance carriers, disability carriers, and workers' compensation carriers. The data need to be received in a standardized format that is easy to transfer between vendors.

This also should be required of third-party administrators that carry enrollment data or enrollment data that sit in an internal system, such as SAP or Oracle. Enrollment data provide information about the numbers of employees enrolled in the benefits program, updated monthly. Validating the enrollment data against the claims data is important in making sure that the foundation of information is established and aligned correctly.

Sometimes enrollment data are commonly separated by business units and individuals within each business unit. If companies look at their claims and enrollment data on a business-unit level, they're looking at them in two systems that are structured differently for how claims payments are allocated. This creates a disconnect in how the finance systems and human resources systems are aligned. Before anything else is integrated, those data need to be brought together accurately and linked into the payroll data.

Companies should be using a consistent technology platform to integrate all of this information by optimizing the investments that have been made in technology throughout the organization. Companies can leverage their enterprise-wide systems to get better visibility into how much they're spending on health care. But the investment in technology has to be made with a vision of how enterprise-wide technology can be optimized to give the entire organization visibility. Even though employers are able to analyze the data to make improvements to their health plan design or their prescription drug benefits, the challenge remains to effectively communicate health-care information to those who need it.

It's important to empower consumers with the right information especially through technology such as personal health records stored online, but when performed outside of the construct of where the health benefits are paid, a split is created in the system. That's the result when platforms ignore the company paying for the health care. If employees are empowered but are not controlling the dollars in terms of what's being paid out, then they are empowered with a great deal of information but no real purchasing power. Employees as consumers need the right tools and help from their employers to bridge that gap.

The components needed to engage employees to become active participants in their health care are similar to the personalized experience consumers have when shopping at Amazon.com. That same level of personalization can occur within privacy laws when individuals complete a personal health record or a health risk assessment. Tag clouds create opportunities to engage the individual with relevant information by using visual representations of word frequencies to generate similar information. Empowering employees means giving them the right technology for personalization that may eventually change behavior.

Consistent Standards Are Necessary

While the digitization of information has greatly advanced, the consistency and standardization of that data haven't maintained the same pace. Certainly, radiology has made leaps in how information is stored and remotely accessed, but consistency and systemization have not yet been implemented across the entire health-care supply chain to create one standard for how information is conveyed between constituents. If the same standards for disseminating information were lacking in the telecom sector, making or receiving a phone call or sending a text message would be difficult. We're able to communicate in real time because every vendor has adopted a standard.

Standards will allow consumers to have access to their electronic medical records and other medical data. Although companies have created microchips, compact discs, and other kinds of devices to compile and store data, it is unclear which format will be the most effective. Before that decision can be made, standardization will have to occur so that information can flow smoothly from providers to insurance carriers, hospitals, and clinics across the country.

Standards will help physicians more fully embrace electronic medical records. Although many have implemented EMRs, other physicians lag behind. More than 20 years ago, as a resident in ophthalmology, I was conducting the research for implementing the first electronic medical records in the ophthalmology department at my university. Since that time, there has been a gradual evolution for how physicians have adopted this technology. For some, it adds a layer of inefficiency to patient visits; for others, it reduces the ability to interact with patients. For smaller practices, the growing overheads and diminishing reimbursements present financial challenges to adoption of the technology.

In contrast, there has been an increase in the number of hospitals that are adopting electronic medical records and electronic billing systems to systematize all of the information that flows through their facilities.

From the insurance carriers' standpoints, they have seen some progress in how they have updated their systems, but there is still much to be done for how they transmit information, how that information is processed, and how it is disseminated. How claims data are processed still varies because of the number of different formats. This results in an inefficient process for transmitting claims data.

First Things First

Before we can get serious about using information technology for improving health care, some fundamental concepts need to be considered in the economics of how health care is purchased. From a health-care-reform and health-care-policy standpoint, it is necessary to create consistent standards for how all health-care data are maintained, encrypted, and transmitted. A system of tax credits needs to be implemented for technology adoption by all of the links in the health-care supply chain to speed the process. The only ways to drive improvement in the cost and quality of health care are by providing the health-care purchaser with transparency into the right metrics and leveraging technology to drive efficiency throughout the market.

Chapter 11—Key Messages

- With a high level of participation by "e-patients" and the trend toward social networking, building interactive health-care social networks is inevitable and will be an integral part of health care in the future: Health 2.0.

- When the platform that drives transparency is connected with where the dollars originate, then companies and their employees will be the beneficiaries.

- Health 2.0 is patient-empowered health care, not consumer-directed health care, and it relies on the interoperability of all health information.

- An ideal platform for the future will revolutionize health care by supporting a social network for health care that serves both benefits companies and their employees.

- Companies need to develop a blueprint for using enterprise-wide systems to integrate human resources, procurement, finance, and other key information.

- Consistent standards need to be developed and implemented to allow medical data to flow smoothly between all of the links in the health-care supply chain.

- The only ways to drive improvements in the cost and quality of health care are by providing transparency into the right metrics and leveraging technology to drive efficiency throughout the market.

Chapter 11—Endnotes

1   Pew Internet Project, "Pew Internet and American Life Project Tracking Surveys," March 2000–May 2008, http://www.pewinternet.org/trends/Internet_Activities_7.22.08.htm.

APPENDIX A

Creating a World-Class Approach to Getting a Company's Health Care *Off the Dime*

The following 11 steps can be used by companies as a blueprint for success:

1. Map your supply chain

Create a map of all of the key constituents that either deliver or purchase health benefits.

2. Define your total cost equation

Gain an understanding of all of the elements involved in providing benefits, not just the direct medical and pharmacy costs but all of the indirect costs, too.

3. Locate all of the data

Identify where all of the data reside and who is required to provide the data in order to complete the total cost equation.

4. Complete the essential triangle

Integrate enrollment data with medical claims data and information in the general ledger to create the foundation for how information can be analyzed.

5. Assure that information is vendor independent

Make sure that analysis is independent of vendors by not using them as the sole source of all of the reporting.

6. List your top priorities

Identify the key elements that are the company's primary focus, whether plan design changes, prescription drug benefit changes, etc.

7. Look for the CURE

Assure access to the cost, utilization, and risk metrics in order to solve the total cost equation.

8. Map metrics for success

Outline the metrics for success of strategies by asking these questions:

- For plan design, how will you measure the risk of a population and how the members are choosing certain health plans?

- For disease management programs, how will you measure outcomes based on risk?

- For prescription drug benefit changes, how will you measure the total cost of making that change in terms of direct and indirect costs and the key metrics?

9. Map to earnings per share (EPS)

Link all metrics to how strategies will impact the company in EPS in order to report back on the performance.

10. Communicate with employees

Connect the dots for employees by communicating information on how they can help manage their health.

11. Close the loop

Conduct an analysis to ascertain whether the programs in which employees are engaged have an impact; fine-tune to bring strategies full circle.

Appendix B

CFO Control Tower

Cost and Utilization Trends

Key Indicators			
Metrics	Jan '06 - Dec '06	Jan '05 - Dec '05	% Change
Employer Medical $	$248,778,313	$238,527,655	4.3%
Employer Rx $	$79,632,261	$74,672,709	6.6%
Employer Medical & Rx $	$328,410,574	$313,200,364	4.9%
Employee Medical $	$29,966,139	$32,633,742	(8.2%)
Employee Rx $	$17,781,585	$18,431,181	(3.5%)
Employee Medical & Rx $	$47,747,724	$51,064,923	(6.5%)
# Employees	46,390	46,526	(0.3%)
# Members	113,073	113,939	(0.8%)
Medical + Rx PEPM	$590	$561	5.2%

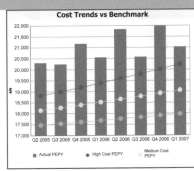

Cost Trends vs Benchmark

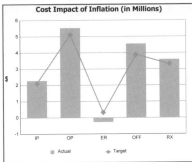

Cost Impact of Inflation (in Millions)

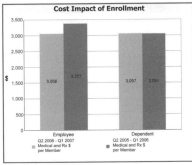

Cost Impact of Enrollment

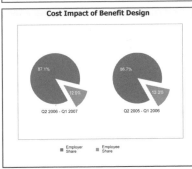

Cost Impact of Benefit Design

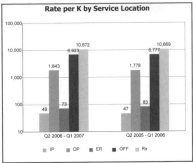

Rate per K by Service Location

CFO Control Tower

Risk Distribution

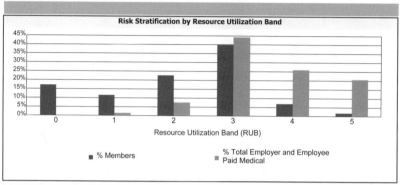

Risk Stratification by Resource Utilization Band

■ % Members

■ % Total Employer and Employee Paid Medical

Total Cost of Members

Member Condition Group (MCG)	Employer Paid Amount Medical $	Employer Paid Amount Rx $	Employer Paid Amount Dental $	Employer Paid Amount Vision $	Employer Paid Amount Disability $	Employer Paid Amount Workers' Compensation $	Total Employer Paid Amount $
Members with Asthma	$18,719,584	$5,076,509	$1,143,076	$157,091	$649,740	$3,836,658	$29,582,657
Members with Cancer	$36,557,764	$4,105,578	$1,115,257	$173,264	$1,763,120	$3,857,530	$47,572,514
Members with Congestive Heart Failure	$15,360,351	$1,313,605	$212,813	$73,936	$580,478	$3,833,365	$21,374,548
Members with Depression	$13,357,955	$3,286,201	$532,383	$121,007	$509,904	$3,844,936	$21,652,391
Members with Diabetes	$31,562,227	$9,059,506	$1,387,462	$280,580	$1,735,767	$4,028,699	$48,054,242
Members with Ischemic Heart Disease or Heart Attack	$27,632,610	$4,471,078	$951,413	$164,051	$1,386,450	$3,897,273	$38,502,875
Members with Low Back Pain	$48,247,345	$10,195,316	$2,824,471	$469,582	$2,768,252	$4,098,044	$68,603,016
Members with Pregnancies, Uncomplicated	$1,170,812	$144,812	$62,586	$4,339	$216,879	$125	$1,599,554
Members with Pregnancies, With Complications	$8,481,727	$408,145	$219,727	$71,110	$870,750	$3,743,105	$13,794,563
Members with Premature Infants	$1,760,258	$9,789	$22	0	$0	0	$1,770,069

Risk Distribution by Business Unit

Organization Level 2	# Members making Medical Claims	Employer Paid Amount Medical $	Co-Morbidity Ratio (Cost)
Corporate	2,289	$8,854,124	0.95
Integrated Defense Systems	13,214	$49,620,863	0.91
Intelligence and Information Systems	8,167	$28,861,767	0.88
Missile Systems	13,416	$39,326,521	0.72
Network Centric Systems	9,036	$36,125,721	0.99
Orphans	2	$14	0.02
Space and Airborne Systems	7,824	$33,353,350	1.08
Specials	9	$84,946	2.33
Vandelay Technical Services Company	4,502	$17,112,408	0.93

CFO Control Tower

Enrollment Trends

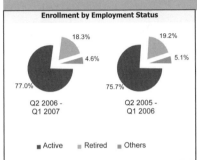

Enrollment by Employment Status

Q2 2006 - Q1 2007: 77.0%, 18.3%, 4.6%

Q2 2005 - Q1 2006: 75.7%, 19.2%, 5.1%

■ Active ■ Retired ■ Others

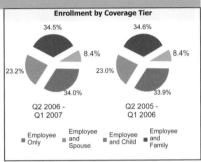

Enrollment by Coverage Tier

Q2 2006 - Q1 2007: 34.5%, 8.4%, 34.0%, 23.2%

Q2 2005 - Q1 2006: 34.6%, 8.4%, 33.9%, 23.0%

■ Employee Only ■ Employee and Spouse ■ Employee and Child ■ Employee and Family

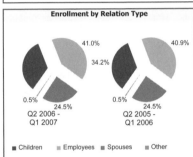

Enrollment by Relation Type

Q2 2006 - Q1 2007: 41.0%, 34.2%, 0.5%, 24.5%

Q2 2005 - Q1 2006: 40.9%, 0.5%, 24.5%

■ Children ■ Employees ■ Spouses ■ Other

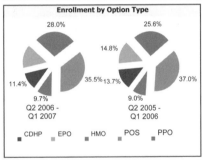

Enrollment by Option Type

Q2 2006 - Q1 2007: 28.0%, 14.8%, 11.4%, 9.7%, 35.5%

Q2 2005 - Q1 2006: 25.6%, 13.7%, 9.0%, 37.0%

■ CDHP ■ EPO ■ HMO ■ POS ■ PPO

Enrollment by Age

Age Sub Group	Q2 2006 - Q1 2007 # Members	Q2 2005 - Q1 2006 # Members
Unknown	59	50
< 1 Year	1,194	1,125
1 - 9 Years	12,273	12,598
10 - 19 Years	21,134	21,502
20 - 44 Years	35,717	36,715
45 - 64 Years	48,928	49,034
65 - 74 Years	12,075	12,998
75 - 84 Years	9,039	9,059
85+ Years	2,280	2,144

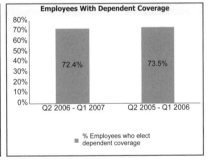

Employees With Dependent Coverage

Q2 2006 - Q1 2007: 72.4%

Q2 2005 - Q1 2006: 73.5%

■ % Employees who elect dependent coverage

251

CFO Control Tower

Drivers of High Medical Spend

Jan '06 - Dec '06	
Top 10 Medical Conditions	
Condition	**Employer Medical $**
Preventive care	$16,290,371
Low back pain	$13,225,544
Benign and unspecified neoplasm	$9,470,356
Ischemic heart disease (excluding acute myocardial infarction)	$8,793,910
Administrative concerns and non-specific laboratory abnormalities	$8,436,466
Degenerative joint disease	$6,877,631
Malignant neoplasms, breast	$6,701,313
Pregnancy and delivery with complications	$6,645,204
Surgical aftercare	$6,463,011
Chest pain	$5,951,022
Top 10 as a % of Overall	**26.3%**

Jan '05 - Dec '05	
Top 10 Medical Conditions	
Condition	**Employer Medical $**
Preventive care	$14,617,738
Low back pain	$12,312,363
Benign and unspecified neoplasm	$9,635,773
Ischemic heart disease (excluding acute myocardial infarction)	$8,840,032
Surgical aftercare	$7,505,106
Malignant neoplasms, breast	$6,816,859
Pregnancy and delivery with complications	$6,685,387
Chest pain	$6,084,368
Degenerative joint disease	$5,660,280
Fractures (excluding digits)	$5,527,681
Top 10 as a % of Overall	**25.0%**

Top 10 Providers		
Provider		**Employer Medical $**
TUCSON MED	6463	$4,177,597
UNIVERSITY	19888	$3,448,096
NORTHWEST	25116	$3,293,251
MEDICAL CI	21727	$3,281,114
MEDICAL CE	19336	$2,646,603
ANCILLARY	125977	$2,611,751
CARONDELET	5451	$2,521,807
RADIOLOGY	28061	$1,996,751
LAHEY CLIN	254555	$1,967,114
BAYLOR MED	4333	$1,882,505
Top 10 as a % of Overall		**8.2%**

Top 10 Providers		
Provider		**Employer Medical $**
TUCSON MED	6463	$3,405,783
NORTHWEST	25116	$3,114,704
MEDICAL CI	21727	$3,067,905
UNIVERSITY	19888	$3,037,237
BAYLOR UNI	28441	$2,925,079
CARONDELET	5451	$2,458,176
BAYLOR MED	4333	$1,802,750
LAHEY CLIN	254555	$1,780,099
RADIOLOGY	28061	$1,774,062
MEDICAL CE	19336	$1,698,501
Top 10 as a % of Overall		**7.5%**

High Cost Members & Claims

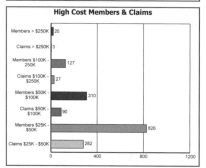

High Cost Members & Claims

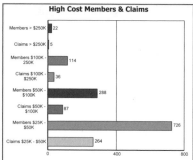

CFO Control Tower

Medical Cost and Utilization Trends

Jan '06 - Dec '06				Jan '05 - Dec '05			
ER Usage Compared to Office Visits				**ER Usage Compared to Office Visits**			
Service Location	Employer $ per Encounter		# Visits	Service Location	Employer $ per Encounter		# Visits
Emergency Room	$899		8,593	Emergency Room	$799		9,774
Office	$113		653,915	Office	$107		632,752

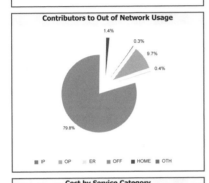

Contributors to Out of Network Usage

1.4%
0.3%
9.7%
0.4%
79.8%

■ IP ■ OP ■ ER ■ OFF ■ HOME ■ OTH

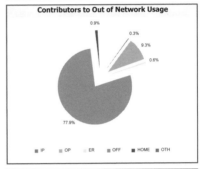

Contributors to Out of Network Usage

0.9%
0.3%
9.3%
0.6%
77.9%

■ IP ■ OP ■ ER ■ OFF ■ HOME ■ OTH

Cost by Service Category		
Service Category	Employer Paid Medical $	Employee Paid Medical $
Medical	$76,995,570	$15,681,904
Surgical	$63,831,808	$4,501,366
Diagnostic and Therapeutic	$51,483,744	$5,953,178
Specialty Rx	$16,859,383	$606,168
Maternity/Newborn	$11,072,739	$866,762
Other	$8,367,089	$200,850
Mental Health/Substance Abuse	$6,970,958	$1,810,615
Emergency Room	$4,285,317	$564,630
Durable Medical Equipment	$4,143,812	$608,485
Ambulance	$1,841,604	$222,116
Home Health	$1,308,280	$87,600
Therapies	$754,240	$62,450
Dialysis Center	$697,272	$77,297
Medical Dental	$540,682	$21,099
Skilled Nursing Facility/Intermediate Care Facility	$176,177	$28,332
Urgent Care Center /Clinic	$159,643	$28,097
Hospice/Respite	$134,675	$5,995
Rehabilitation	$108,407	$8,567
Medical Vision	$49,450	$10,302
Day/Night Treatment	$10,798	$919
Unknown	($1,013,334)	($1,380,592)
Total	$248,778,313	$29,966,139

Cost by Service Category		
Service Category	Employer Paid Medical $	Employee Paid Medical $
Medical	$74,206,873	$15,706,872
Surgical	$56,828,059	$5,121,428
Diagnostic and Therapeutic	$47,991,211	$6,049,447
Specialty Rx	$18,331,194	$740,202
Maternity/Newborn	$10,377,301	$817,711
Other	$9,171,164	$1,305,200
Mental Health/Substance Abuse	$6,680,513	$1,805,932
Emergency Room	$4,599,695	$694,079
Durable Medical Equipment	$3,946,319	$627,214
Ambulance	$1,958,553	$147,551
Home Health	$1,159,597	$210,406
Therapies	$925,687	$51,019
Dialysis Center	$767,416	$186,782
Unknown	$568,232	($878,629)
Medical Dental	$407,043	$12,852
Skilled Nursing Facility/Intermediate Care Facility	$150,412	$2,861
Rehabilitation	$138,387	$1,343
Urgent Care Center /Clinic	$129,217	$20,254
Hospice/Respite	$101,452	$2,059
Medical Vision	$61,514	$5,107
Day/Night Treatment	$27,818	$4,052
Total	$238,527,655	$32,633,742

253

CFO Control Tower

Pharmacy Cost and Utilization Trends

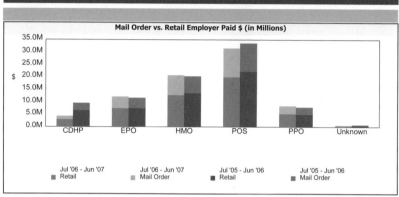

Mail Order vs. Retail Employer Paid $ (in Millions)

Jul '06 - Jun '07
■ Retail

Jul '06 - Jun '07
■ Mail Order

Jul '05 - Jun '06
■ Retail

Jul '05 - Jun '06
■ Mail Order

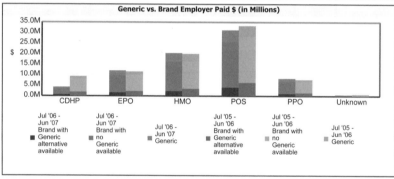

Generic vs. Brand Employer Paid $ (in Millions)

Jul '06 - Jun '07
■ Brand with Generic alternative available

Jul '06 - Jun '07
■ no Generic available

Jul '06 - Jun '07
■ Generic

Jul '05 - Jun '06
■ Brand with Generic alternative available

Jul '05 - Jun '06
■ no Generic available

Jul '05 - Jun '06
■ Generic

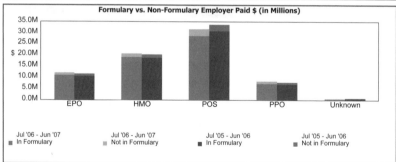

Formulary vs. Non-Formulary Employer Paid $ (in Millions)

Jul '06 - Jun '07
■ In Formulary

Jul '06 - Jun '07
■ Not in Formulary

Jul '05 - Jun '06
■ In Formulary

Jul '05 - Jun '06
■ Not in Formulary

CFO Control Tower

Drivers of High Pharmacy Spend

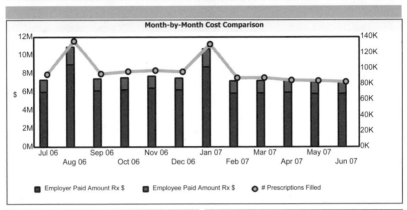

Month-by-Month Cost Comparison

■ Employer Paid Amount Rx $ ■ Employee Paid Amount Rx $ ● # Prescriptions Filled

Top 10 Drugs: Jul '06 - Jun '07	
Drug	Employer Paid Amount Rx $
LIPITOR	$3,534,920
NEXIUM	$3,424,332
ENBREL	$2,086,572
SINGULAIR	$1,394,336
ADVAIR DISKUS	$1,370,758
EFFEXOR XR	$1,112,037
SIMVASTATIN	$989,503
HUMIRA	$904,519
TOPAMAX	$821,550
ZYRTEC	$809,129
Top 10 as a % of Overall	20.8%

Top 10 Drugs: Jul '05 - Jun '06	
Drug	Employer Paid Amount Rx $
LIPITOR	$7,505,298
NEXIUM	$5,054,783
ZOCOR	$4,074,408
ENBREL	$2,556,075
ADVAIR DISKUS	$2,280,064
ZOLOFT	$1,765,373
PROTONIX	$1,734,238
EFFEXOR XR	$1,707,665
SINGULAIR	$1,644,548
PLAVIX	$1,626,011
Top 10 as a % of Overall	23.0%

CFO Control Tower

Claims Recovery

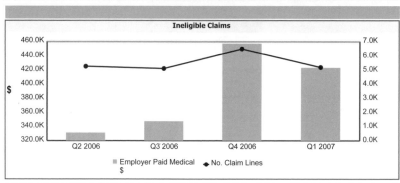

Ineligible Claims

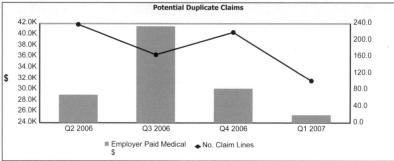

Potential Duplicate Claims

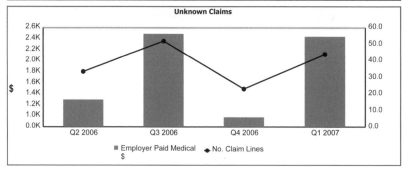

Unknown Claims

INDEX

Page numbers in italics refer to figures and tables.